METAPHYSICS

A CRITICAL SURVEY OF ITS MEANING

METAPHYSICS

A CRITICAL SURVEY OF ITS MEANING

by

TAKATURA ANDO

Professor of Philosophy at Ritumekan University, Kyoto

Second enlarged edition

THE HAGUE

MARTINUS NIJHOFF

1974

First edition 1963

FOREWORD

In the summer of 1960 I visited Oxford and stayed there several months. This book was written as some slight memorial of my days in that ancient seat of learning. It is my pleasant duty to acknowledge the great debt I own to Mr. D. Lyness in the task of putting it into English. In addition I remember with gratitude Dr. J. L. Ackrill of Brasenose College, who gave me unfailing encouragement, and also Dr. R. A. Rees of Jesus College, who read my manuscript through and subjected it to a minute revision. Lastly for permission to quote from Sir W. D. Ross' translation of Aristotle's Metaphysics, I have to thank the editors of Oxford University Press.

Kyoto, Japan   T. A.
Sep. 1961.

To answer the readers' complaints that the first edition did not explain the author's attitude towards metaphysics, one more chapter on new positivism was written in 1966, but the publication was delayed till the second edition. Special thanks are due to Mr. E. B. Brooks for his assistance in writing English, to Prof. Philip P. Wiener, and to Dr. R. A. Rees, both for some kind services.

Okayama 1973   T. A.

CONTENTS

INTRODUCTION

No science is subject to such contrary evaluations as metaphysics. Sometimes it is called the queen of all the sciences, sometimes it is outcast and forsaken like Hecuba. [1] The evaluation has changed several times even since Kant. In the present situation, the number of its admirers is matched by the number of its denigrators, and the final outcome hardly seems to be predictable. Such instability is admittedly natural to a position of great honour. But the problem is not, as Kant considered it, just a matter of the ability of metaphysics to perform its task. What is most perplexing is that we cannot find any single definition of metaphysics common to both its admirers and its denigrators. This, I think, is the most important reason why there has been no correct evaluation of metaphysics. The neglect of definition which, as Socrates maintained, should be the primary subject of philosophy, has resulted in many of the disputes of contemporary philosophy. So as to shed some light on this confusion, the present inquiry aims at a concise survey of the usage of the term metaphysics. Metaphysics must not be defined *a priori;* we must reach a definition inductively from the history of metaphysics. For we have without doubt a history of thought which is called metaphysics. An *a priori* concept, which ignores this history, cannot claim universal validity. Even when one wishes to express a completely original thought, one is not allowed to neglect the history of the concepts one employs.

The history of metaphysics either covers the whole history of philosophy or at least forms more than half of it. But a History of Metaphysics cannot explain the concept of metaphysics itself. In order to make a History of Metaphysics out of the whole of philosophy, one must implicitly presuppose a definition of metaphysics. Therefore, a classification of what philosophers meant by the term must precede a History of Metaphysics. This is just what this inquiry aims at. A comprehensive enumeration of historical usages would not necessarily be effective. Such a task should be entrusted to a lexicon of philosophy.

Kant, *K.d.r.V.*, Vorrede.

Our scope must be limited to the most important usages. It is not certain whether the various usages may be reduced to a single meaning or whether they form a continuous series of development. Any metaphysical presupposition must be strictly prohibited. The attempt to arrive at a systematic explanation is of course of extreme importance. But it must be preceded by plain observation of historical facts.

CHAPTER I

THE ORIGIN OF THE CONCEPT OF METAPHYSICS

I. REINER'S THEORY

The concept metaphysics originates from the Greek words τὰ μετὰ τὰ φυσικά, which is the name of a work by Aristotle. There is a traditional explanation of this name which has been universally accepted. The main work of Aristotle which has come to be called *metaphysica*, or more strictly speaking the essential part of that work, was called by Aristotle himself πρώτη φιλοσοφία, θεολογική, or merely σοφία. The title "metaphysics" originated later, viz. when Andronicus of Rhodes, a Peripatetic in the first century B.C., published the complete works of Aristotle, and placed this book after physical treatises. Originally it was not a complete work written continuously but was made up of several lectures delivered in different periods, and the author did not give it a definite title. Andronicus, therefore, embarrassed at the lack of a suitable title, called it τὰ μετὰ τὰ φυσικά, which means the books placed after physical treatises; hence came the word metaphysics. Now, as the word μετά may also mean *trans*, the term metaphysics might have come to mean the science concerned with transcendent reality or intelligible being, and so by chance suited the content of the first philosophy. This seemingly reasonable explanation, though uncritically accepted by most philosophers and historians and admitted as orthodox, appears to be a little far-fetched. For it would have been too much of a coincidence for the concept metaphysics, which originally indicated a mere editorial sequence, to be successfully adapted so as to contain the science of transcendent reality. Kant actually declared his suspicion saying that the expression is too felicitous to be regarded as the result of chance. [1] It is not really an exaggeration to call it a scandal, as Max Wundt is reported to have done, that modern philosophers paid no serious attention to this point. Hans Reiner, [2] therefore, deserves the highest praise for recently pointing out

---

[1] M. Heinze, *Vorlesungen Kants über Metaphysik aus drei Semestern*, 1894, S. 186. (Abhand. d. Sächs. Akad. d. Wiss. XIV. Nr. VI. phil. -hist. Klasse, p. 666)
[2] Hans Reiner, 'Die Entstehung und ursprüngliche Bedeutung des Namens Metaphysik.' (*Zeitschr. f. philosoph. Forsch.* VIII. 2. 1954)

this misinterpretation and explaining the real origin of the word metaphysics.

According to Reiner, it would have been a quite arbitrary procedure to christen the science, which Aristotle himself called the first philosophy, and Theophrastus the first theology, with a name derived by chance from the mere editorial sequence of the work. The interpretations of this book by Alexander of Aphrodisias and by Asclepius, on which modern scholars like Brandis, Zeller, and Bonitz base the above mentioned hypothesis, tell us in reality, that the book was called τὰ μετὰ τὰ φυσικά, because it came after the physical sciences. Rather than mentioning anything about its origin from Andronicus' arbitrary arrangement, Alexander and Asclepius said that the order was τάξις πρὸς ἡμᾶς. Anyone who has learned a little about Aristotle's philosophy must know that πρὸς ἡμᾶς ὕστερον is the contradictory opposite of πρὸς ἡμᾶς πρότερον, which on its side, is the contrary of φύσει πρότερον. Metaphysics is posterior to physical sciences in the order in which we learn things, and this is consistent with calling metaphysics πρώτη φιλοσοφία, first philosophy, i.e., prior in the order of being. Bonitz quotes also from Themistius and Simplicius. But the former quotation refers to the distinction between πρὸς ἡμᾶς and τῇ φύσει, while the latter mentions the Platonic interpretation of μετὰ τὰ φυσικά, viz. the transcendency of the object of metaphysics beyond nature – ὑπὲρ φύσιν, ἐπέκεινα τῶν φυσικῶν. Neither of these quotations can prove the interpretation of the bibliographical origin of the term.

The name *metaphysica*, Reiner proceeds, cannot be found even in Diogenes Laertius, the oldest catalogue of Aristotle's works. The first person to use this title is Nicolaus of Damascus, who lived in the latter half of the first century B.C. In a commentary on Theophrastus' *metaphysics* – this book had also originally another name – we find that Nicolaus of Damascus wrote a book on Aristotle's μετὰ τὰ φυσικά. Alexander of Aphrodisias is connected, on the one hand, to Andronicus of Rhodes through Adrastus of Aphrodisias, and on the other, to Nicolaus through Alexander, so that the origin of his interpretation can be traced back to Andronicus and Nicolaus. Seeing that Averroes and Avicenna, who must have been acquainted with the book by Nicolaus, also maintain the interpretation by Alexander and Asclepius, it may safely be inferred that Nicolaus agreed with them. So the editorial order by Andronicus must be construed as expressly following the order in which we learn things. According to the general inclination of the Peripatetics towards empiricism, Andronicus also might have attached a lot of importance to educational order, which Aristotle called πρὸς ἡμᾶς, and assuming the name πρώτη φιλοσοφία to be unsuitable to this science he might have preferred the name μετὰ τὰ φυσικά. But the name is not his invention; it must be traced back earlier. Though as we have already said we cannot find it in the list of Diogenes Laertius, it seems very probable that it was included in an earlier list – that of Hermippus (ca. 200 B.C.) – and was by some chance dropped from the list of Diogenes. According to Howald, Ariston of Ceus who was master of the Peripatetic school from 228–5 B.C., made a list of philosophical works before Hermippus and Diogenes presumably used this when he made his list.

The origin of the name of metaphysics, thus traced back to one century after Aristotle's death, might be safely conjectured to reflect the sequence which Aristotle himself followed. The name 'first philosophy' is due to the Platonic line of thought characteristic of Aristotle's early period. When Aristotle in later years inclined to empirical thought, the order πρὸς ἡμᾶς πρότερον became the predominant principle of his philosophy. One piece of evidence for this is the fact that his metaphysics quotes the other works most often.

Eudemus, Aristotle's immediate disciple, the author of the *History of Theology*, and the first editor of his teacher's works, is supposed by Reimer to have invented the name τὰ μετὰ τὰ φυσικά. Reiner also conjectures that as well as indicating its educational position next to the physical treatises, the word had for Eudemus the Platonic meaning, 'μετ' ἐκεῖνα, ἐπέκεινα' appropriate to his inclination to Platonism. When Eudemus edited the works, the science which from a Platonic standpoint Aristotle called the first philosophy, was attached to other relevant treatises, and was given the title τὰ μετὰ τὰ φυσικά. Andronicus followed Eudemus and preferred the name μεταφυσικά because he considered the original name of 'first philosophy' to be unsuitable to educational order. In doing this Andronicus was following orthodox Aristotelianism, so, Reiner concludes, we must reject the hypothesis of the accidental bibliographical origin of the term.

Reiner's theory seems to me quite persuasive and his proof is sufficient to dispel the long-standing mistake about the origin of the word 'metaphysics.' The word 'metaphysics' did not originate from somebody's being at a loss as to what to call a book, but rather, as Kant suggested, is the most suitable designation of the first philosophy, a concept presumably based on the orthodox tradition from Aristotle and his immediate followers.

Reiner [1] also explained in detail how the misinterpretation came to be accepted. According to him, Aristotle's metaphysics was first made known to the mediaeval world when it was mentioned in the commentary on the *De Interpretatione* by Boethius, a contemporary of Asclepius. But, at this time, only the name of μετὰ τὰ φυσικά came to be known. It was not until the middle of the twelfth century, that the contents of the book became familiar and the problem of the meaning of the title was noticed. Dominicus Gundissalinus, in his *De Divisione Philosophiae*, which was published in 1150, gives Alexander's interpretation, saying that the book is posterior not in itself but for us. This is also the opinion of Avicenna, an Arabian who translated Metaphysics into Latin, and his fellow countryman Averroes. Though Albertus Magnus and Thomas Aquinas tended to take the *metaphysica* as *transphysica* rather than as *postphysica*, they did not give up the interpretation of Alexander and Avicenna. These two kinds of interpretation were inherited by later Scholastics. The theory, which later became so widespread that the name *metaphysica* was derived from the editorial sequence of Andronicus, was initiated by Franciscus Patricius' *Discussiones Peripateticae I*. Not being well acquainted with Greek Interpretations, he decided that Andronicus gave this title to the book through dissatisfaction with the Aristotelian title of 'first philosophy' or 'theology.' The reason why Patricius came to this conclusion was that the name 'metaphysics' is not to be found in either Aristotle or Diogenes Laertius, but only appears in Nicolaus and Plutarch. The theory that the name resulted from a mere editorial sequence, and that the book *Metaphysics* did not originally form a single work, was first set forth in Buhle's *Ueber die Aechtheit der Metaphysik des Aristotles* 1788. It was adopted by Harless in his edition of Fabricius' *Bibliotheca Graeca*, ed. 4. 1793, and the wide dispersal of this book caused the theory to become so dominant that even the great nineteenth century historians of philosophy, like Brandis, Zeller, and Bonitz accepted it uncritically.

2. ARISTOTLE'S METAPHYSICS

Seeing that the concept of metaphysics is derived from a work of Aristotle, and that the title of this work reflects the author's design, being chosen, if not by the author himself, at least by his immediate

---

[1] H. Reiner, 'Die Entstehung der Lehre vom bibliothekarischen Ursprung des Namens Metaphysik.' (*Z. f. ph. F. IX. I. 1955*)

disciples, we must first analyse Aristotle's *Metaphysics* as a preliminary to tracing the historical development of this concept and of the knowledge which has been called with this name. On the basis of this historical study we hope to reach some conclusion as to the possibility and legitimacy of metaphysics.

Aristotle's *Metaphysics*, as it has come down to us, is made up of fourteen volumes each containing a short treatise. But in the Anonymus Menagii list, it was described as μεταφυσικά K, i.e. metaphysica in ten volumes. These ten volumes were, so Ross [1] conjectures, A, B, Γ, E, Z, H, θ, I, M, and N, the four volumes α, Δ, K, and Λ being omitted. In a note to the oldest codex E, α is attributed to Pasicles of Rhodes, a disciple of Aristotle and nephew of Eudemus. Ross and Jaeger [2] confirm this attribution. Δ is generally considered to be an early work of Aristotle's, not originally belonging to the metaphysics and even earlier than the physical treatises which precede all the other parts of the metaphysics. K is made up of two parts: $1059^{a18} - 1065^{a26}$, and $1065^{a26} - 1069^{a12}$. The former part is a concise description of the content of B, Γ, and E, and the second is composed of extracts from Phys. II, III, and IV. According to Ross, the first is a note made by a disciple at an earlier date than B, Γ, E, and the second though it may be the work of a disciple, is more probably Aristotle's own work. Λ is an independent treatise and is generally assumed to be an early work. But chapter 8 (except 1074^{a31-38}), in which the cosmology of Callippus and Eudoxus is dealt with, must be later than 330–325 B.C. For this reason Jaeger explained this part to be an addition made by Aristotle himself. Mansion [3] and Nuyens [4] maintained that Λ belonged to a later period, but anyhow, the four books, α, Δ, K, and Λ may safely be assumed not to have been included in the ten volumes of the Anonymus Menagii list.

It may be that the other ten books were not written continuously and that the whole work is a compilation of several independent treatises. The ten books are divided into four parts: ABΓE, ZHθ, MN, and I. Brandis and Bonitz considered the three books of the second group to be the main part of the metaphysics. But according to Jaeger the original metaphysics was composed of A, K ($- 1065^{a26}$), M ($1086^{a21} -$),

---

[1] W. D. Ross, *Aristotle's Metaphysics*, 1924. Introd.

[2] W. Jaeger, *Aristoteles: Grundlegung einer Geschichte seiner Entwicklung*, 1923.

[3] A. Mansion, 'La genèse de l'oeuvre d'Aristote d'après les travaux récents.' (*Revue Néoscholastique de philosophie*, XXXIX, 1927)

[4] F. Nuyens, *L'évolution de la psychologie d'Aristotle*. Ouvrage traduit du Néerlandais, 1948.

and N; B, Γ, and E is a revision of K (– 1065^{a26}); and M (– 1086^{a21}) is the new form of M (1086^{a21}) and N while I is an independent treatise. These treatises, written at different times, were put together, firstly, the four groups of ABΓE, ZHθ, MN, and I; afterwards the four books, α, Δ, K, and Λ, were added to this compilation and thus the present *Metaphysics* in fourteen books was formed. This has been the orthodox theory of how the *Metaphysics* was constructed.

Nuyens, who tried to determine the dates of Aristotle's works from a new point of view, differed from Jaeger over the physical and psychological treatises. But with the metaphysics, he follows as a rule Jaeger's opinion, except with regard to Z, H, θ, and Λ. In relation to the development of the concept ψύχη, which Nuyens adopted as a standard for dating Aristotle's works, Z, H, and θ are later than Jaeger thought, and belong to Aristotle's last period. Nuyens also puts Λ in this period, but in this he disagrees with Jaeger and Ross. This difference of opinion is highly relevant to the problem of determining the essence of metaphysics. For Z, H, θ, and Λ are the most important parts of metaphysics, ZHθ being concerned with being in general, and Λ with divine being; and if Jaeger is right and these two groups belong to different periods, we infer that Aristotle's view of metaphysics changed during these periods. But if Mansion and Nuyens are right, we can make no such inference. Jaeger and Nuyens use different methods of dating, and it is difficult to choose between them. This, I think, is a limitation of philological method. But without concerning ourselves too much with this *aporia*, let us accept Aristotle's metaphysics in its present form and search in it for the essence of his metaphysics. This is by no means an evasion of a difficult task, as might be suspected. For if as Jaeger considers, the two main groups of ZHθ and Λ, were both outside the original *Metaphysics*, the *Metaphysics* as we have it, i.e. the *Metaphysics* in the history of philosophy, would be completely excluded from the original *Metaphysics*. And our problem is not to date Aristotle's works, but rather to find an historical definition of metaphysics. So if we go too far into this philological discussion, we shall lose more than we gain.

Aristotle called metaphysics by at least three different names: σοφία, πρώτη φιλοσοφία, and θεολογική. How then did he use these concepts and what was the relation between them? In E.N. VI σοφία is put amongst the intellectual virtues with τέχνη, φρόνησις, ἐπιστήμη, and νοῦς. It is explained as the knowledge with a head, (κεφαλὴν ἔχουσα) [1] concerning most noble things. By noble things he means

---

[1] *Eth. Nic.* VI. 7. 1141a18.

eternal and necessary being as the object of ἐπιστήμη, and by the head, νοῦς, the faculty of conceiving final principles. Thus, σοφία is considered in the *Ethics* to be a kind of theoretical knowledge of necessary and eternal being, both intuitive and inferential.

As this definition of σοφία is quoted in Met. A., [1] we can assume that Aristotle used this same concept in essentially the same way in the *Metaphysics*. Now, at the beginning of the *Metaphysics*, [2] there is a discussion about the kinds and stages of knowledge: – Human knowledge originates from sensation and develops gradually into memory, experience, and art. In this development, σοφία i.e. wisdom, is the highest scientific knowledge and deals with the principles or causes of things. This is proved by the fact that a person who is generally called σοφός (wise) possesses the following characteristics: he knows, (1) everything, though not in detail, (2) the most difficult things, (3) what is most exact, (4) what best explains how things happen, (5) things for their own sake, and (6) for what end everything is done. All of these characteristics of the wise man are the expression of σοφία as general knowledge about causes.

The objects of σοφία are principles and causes; the good and the end (τέλος) are its special form. With regard to the attitude of the knower, σοφία is knowledge for its own sake without any utilitarian interest. This is not a characteristic confined to highly advanced philosophy; even the love of myth may be regarded as a sign of a philosophical attitude. φιλοσοφία, the love of knowledge for its own sake, is the knowledge suitable for those who live free and independent lives. σοφία, the system of philosophy, is the result of this disinterested love of knowledge. Strictly speaking, such knowledge is more suitable for the Gods than for mankind. It is divine in two ways; firstly, because God is the cause of everything and is the first principle with which this science is concerned, and secondly, because either God alone or God above all can have such knowledge. In other words God is both object and subject of σοφία.

There is no doubt that the σοφία mentioned above means philosophy proper rather than science in general. But it is not certain whether it means philosophy in general or whether it refers especially to metaphysics – first philosophy. The characteristics of the σοφός enumerated above seem to be common to all philosophical sciences; however, from the last mentioned divine character of its object and subject, σοφία

[1] *Met. A.* I. 981b25.
[2] *Met. A.* I. 2.

must be limited to first philosophy, or metaphysics as theology.

The objects, problems, and method of σοφία are investigated more minutely in Met. B, Γ, and E. What is in these books called ἡ ἐπιζητουμένη ἐπιστήμη, the science we are seeking, is just this kind of knowledge. The ἐπιστήμη here seems to indicate knowledge in general rather than a moment of σοφία. When we read at the beginning of Γ, "There is a science which investigates being as being..." it appears, at first glance, as if we have struck quite a new idea. But it soon becomes clear that it is nothing more than a detailed explanation of σοφία. "Now this is not the same science as any of the so-called special sciences, for none of these others treat universally of being as being. They cut off a part of being and investigate the attributes of this part; mathematical sciences for instance do. Now since we are seeking the first principles and supreme causes, clearly there must be something to which these belong in virtue of its own nature. If then those who sought the elements of existing things were seeking these same principles, it is necessary that the elements must be elements of being not by accident but just because it is being." What deserves special notice is that the σοφία, which was explained before as the universal knowledge of principles and causes, is now defined as the investigation of being *qua* being, and that the special sciences like mathematics are excluded from this knowledge. What is then the science of being as being? Is it really metaphysics as general ontology?

Expounding this problem, Met. Γ. 2. points out that there are many different meanings of the word 'being,' but each is related to a central meaning, and this central meaning of 'being' is 'substance.' Thus, "It is clear then that it is the work of one science also to study the things that are, *qua* being. But everywhere science deals chiefly with that which is primary, and on which the other things depend, and in virtue of which they get their names. If, then, this is substance, it will be of substances that the philosopher must grasp the principles and the causes."

We find here that Aristotle either identifies the science of being *qua* being with the science of principles and causes of substances, or he moves from one to the other. [1] Further, the last sentence of the above

---

[1] The argument in K, which is the old form of ΒΓE, is similar to the new *Metaphysics*. No essential difference can be seen, except in K 3,1061a8, which corresponds to B2,1003b1, the central being to which every other being is referred is called being *qua* being without substituting 'substance' for it. Also in 1061a 30ff., philosophy is characterised as the science which deals with being *qua* being, abstracting all its attributes, just as mathematics abstracts the sensible qualities of the object and deals only with quantity and continuity. In this respect philosophy is distinguished from physics, dialectic, and sophistic, which deal

quotation may be taken in two different senses. It may be taken to mean either that philosophy is generically one and is divided into species according to its different objects, or that philosophy deals with being in general, while other sciences deal with special beings. The statement in 1004ᵃ3 seems to support the former interpretation: "And there are as many parts of philosophy as there are kinds of substance, so that there must necessarily be among them a first philosophy and one which follows this. For being falls immediately into genera; for which reason the sciences too will correspond to the genera. Hence the philosopher is told just like the mathematician. For mathematics also has its parts, and in this science also there is some primary science, another secondary science, and other subsequent sciences."

This is evidently an argument which would apply the principle of dividing science according to its objects to philosophy, whereby the classification of mathematical sciences is used as its analogical pattern. Herewith the preparation is made for the specific concept πρώτη φιλοσοφία, as a kind of σοφία or φιλοσοφία. 1

with other accidental attributes. But there is also no attempt to identify the science of being *qua* being with the science of substance. If philosophy is regarded as the science of substance, it may be divided into parts which correspond to the species of substance with which it is concerned, and physics may be a part of philosophy since it is the science of sensible substances. It would be too much to say that the idea of taking substance to be the centre to which other beings are referred appeared first in the new *Metaphysics*. But at least this idea remained implicit in the old *Metaphysics*, so that the difficulties which concern metaphysics as a universal science and metaphysics as the science of special substance did not come to light.

1 K 4, the old form of Γ 2–3, is almost the same as this; cf. 1061b17ff: "Since even the mathematician uses the common axioms only in a special application, it must be the business of first philosophy to examine the principles of mathematics also. That when equals are taken from equals the remainders are equal, is common to all quantities, but mathematics studies a part of its proper matter which it has detached, e.g. lines or angles or numbers or some other kind of quantity – not, however, *qua* being but in so far as each of them is continuous in one or two or three dimensions; but philosophy does not inquire about particular subjects in so far as each of them has some attribute or other, but speculates about being, in so far as each particular thing is. – Physics is in the same position as mathematics; for physics studies the attributes and the principles of things that are, *qua* moving and not *qua* being (whereas the primary science, we have said, deals with these only in so far as the underlying subjects are existent, and not in virtue of any other character); and so both physics and mathematics must be classed as parts of wisdom." If physics and mathematics are parts of σοφία, they must be kinds of philosophy. But according to the argument in this chapter, philosophy deals with being *qua* being, while physics and mathematics deal with special being. Therefore 'philosophy' here must be taken in two senses, either as genus or as species. And if physics and mathematics are the sciences of special being, σοφία, which is the genus of these sciences, must be taken as science in a wider sense, or at least as theoretical science in general. The word πρώτη ἐπιστήμη seems to suggest this. But if we take σοφία as philosophy in the proper sense, physics and mathematics, which form the parts of this σοφία must be something like what was previously called universal mathematics instead of being sciences of mere special beings. The science which deals with mathematical principles such as "When equals are taken from equals, the remainders are equal" is mathematical philosophy, which will coincide with universal mathematics.

Against the possible suspicion that this would not be consistent with making philosophy a science of substance, Aristotle explains that it is not unbecoming for philosophy to deal with attributes, if one holds that substance is the first being to which every attribute belongs. So, the consideration of accidental attributes in reference to substance, is what distinguishes a (true) philosophical inquiry from the methods of the sophists and the dialecticians.

The philosophy which deals with being *qua* being, is identified with the science of substance. Philosophy does not however, inquire into substance apart from attributes, it also deals with attributes in combination with substance. In this respect, philosophy may be regarded indirectly as the science of all things. "And for this reason it does not belong to the geometer to inquire what is contrariety or completeness or unity or being or the same or the other, but only to presuppose these concepts and reason from this starting-point. Obviously then it is the work of one science to examine being *qua* being, and the attributes which belong to it *qua* being, and the same science will examine not substances but also their attributes, both those above named and the concepts 'prior' and 'posterior,' 'genus' and 'species,' 'whole' and 'part,' and the others of this sort... We must state whether it belongs to one or to different sciences to inquire into the truths which are in mathematics called axioms, and into substance. Evidently, the inquiry into these also belongs to one science, and that the science of the philosopher; for these truths hold good for everything that is, and not for some special genus apart from others... And for this reason no one who is conducting a special inquiry tries to say anything about their truth or falsity, – neither the geometer nor the arithmetician. Some natural philosophers indeed have done so, and their procedure was intelligible enough; for they thought that they alone were inquiring about the whole of nature and about being. But since there is one kind of thinker who is above even the natural philosopher (for nature is only one particular genus of being), the discussion of these truths also will belong to him whose inquiry is universal and deals with primary substance. Physics also is a kind of wisdom, but it is not the first kind."

Thus it was argued that to inquire into being *qua* being is not different from inquiring into everything with reference to substance or from inquiring into universal principles of being. φυσική is also acknowledged to be a kind of σοφία. σοφία in this context seems to imply philosophy in general, for πρώτη φιλοσοφία is mentioned over and above φυσική. Further, we may infer from the above statement that if there is πρώτη φιλοσοφία at all, it must be "a universal inquiry and science of the first substance." Hence we learn that the science of being *qua* being is the science of substance, especially of the first substance. – But why, above all, of the first substance and not substance in general? This question concerns the relationship between ontology and theology.

The same problem of the general and the particular is resumed in Met. E. 1., where the science of being *qua* being, or the science of cause and principle, is distinguished from the special sciences. A special science deals with some particular being without investigating its essence, making it plain to the senses, and putting forward its existence as a hypothesis. It does not ask whether or not its object really exists. The philosophy which deals with being *qua* being has entirely opposite characteristics to those of the special science mentioned above. It is the science which deals with being in general as a whole, and inquires into essence and reality.

After this, Aristotle goes on to distinguish theoretical, practical and productive knowledge. Theoretical knowledge is subdivided according to its objects into physics, mathematics and theology. There are various kinds of substance. In the first place those which are movable and inseparable from matter. These are the objects of physics. In the second place, those which are immovable but inseparable from matter. Mathematics is concerned with these substances. In the third place, those, if any, which are eternal, immovable, and separable from matter. The science which deals with such objects obviously belongs to theoretical knowledge like physics and mathematics, but it is different from them and is πρώτη ἐπιστήμη, i.e. the first science. Thus Aristotle concludes that there are three kinds of φιλοσοφίαι θεωρητικαί, viz. μαθηματική, φυσική, θεολογική. Of these three, theology is the highest science and deals with the highest class. [1]

---

[1] The statement in K 7, is almost the same as that in E 1. It runs as follows: 1063b35ff. "Every science seeks certain principles and causes for each of its objects – e.g. medicine and gymnastics... There is a science of nature, and evidently it must be different both from practical and from productive science. For in the case of productive science the principle of movement is in the producer and not in the product, and is either an art or some other faculty... But the science of the natural philosopher deals with the things that have in themselves a principle of movement. It is clear from these facts, then, that natural science must be neither practical nor productive, but theoretical... Since there is a science of being *qua* being and capable of existing apart, we must consider whether this is to be regarded as the same as physics or as different. Physics deals with the things that have a principle of movement in themselves; mathematics is theoretical, and is a science that deals with things that are at rest, but its subjects cannot exist apart. Therefore about that which can exist apart and is unmovable there is a science different from both of these, if there is a substance of this nature (I mean separable and unmovable), as we shall try to prove there is. And if there is such a kind of thing in the world, here must surely be the divine, and this must be the first and most dominant principle. Evidently, then, there are three kinds of theoretical science –

Needless to say, theology is the highest ἐπιστήμη as well as the highest φιλοσοφία. But what is the precise meaning of φιλοσοφία if physics and mathematics are to be included in φιλοσοφίαι θεωρητικαί? If it is the science which deals with being as being, it cannot possibly include mathematics or physics. There are two possible ways of avoiding this contradiction: we can either take φιλοσοφία, which includes mathematics and physics together with theology, as merely synonymous with ἐπιστήμη, [1] or we can divide mathematics and physics into universal and particular and make the former φιλοσοφίαι θεωρητικαί. Of these two alternatives, the latter seems to be the more plausible. φιλοσοφία is theoretical knowledge of universal principles rather than ἐπιστήμη in general. To it belongs the science of physical and mathematical principles. But there are also besides these, the special and applied parts of physics and mathematics.

However, even if general mathematics and general physics are concerned with universal principles, as far as they are mathematics and physics, the science which includes these branches of theoretical science cannot be regarded as being quite the same as the science of being *qua* being. At least theology is not the same as the former science, because theology is also a special branch of theoretical science. If first philosophy is identified with theology, [2] then philosophy as a genus will be a

physics, mathematics, theology. The class of theoretical sciences is the best, and of these themselves the last named is best; for it deals with the highest of existing things, and each science is called better or worse in virtue of its proper object. One might raise the question whether the science of being *qua* being is to be regarded as universal or not. Each of the mathematical sciences deals with some one determinate class of things, but universal mathematics applies alike to all. Now if natural substances are the first of existing things, physics must be the first of sciences; but if there is another entity and substance, separable and un-movable, the knowledge of it must be different and prior to physics and universal because it is prior." The argument agrees almost completely with the argument in E I. The only difference is that here the genus of physics, mathematics and theology is called θεωρητικὴ ἐπιστήμη instead of θεωρητικὴ φιλοσοφία and, instead of asking whether πρώτη φιλοσοφία is universal or not, Aristotle asks whether the ἐπιστήμη which deals with being *qua* being is universal or not. In K, physics and mathematics are not called branches of φιλοσοφία, but are regarded as branches of theoretical ἐπιστήμη. We may infer from this that the idea that mathematics and physics are a kind of philosophy is later, and that in the old *Metaphysics* these two are considered to be theoretical sciences. In other words, philosophy and science were more sharply divided in the old *Metaphysics*. But what is more probable is that θεωρη-τικὴ ἐπιστήμη and θεωρητικὴ φιλοσοφία were used almost synonymously in both cases.

[1] Plato not a few times used φιλοσοφία to mean science in general e.g. *Theaet.* 143 D. "Geometry or other φιλοσοφία." In Aristotle, φιλοσοφία in the wider sense is almost syn-onymous with ἐπιστήμη and includes even practical or productive knowledge.

[2] The term πρώτη φιλοσοφία naturally presupposes δευτέρα φιλοσοφία which is in fact the same as φυσική. Now if 'first philosophy' is to mean ontology, which deals with being *qua* being, in its universal form, the term 'second philosophy' is inappropriate. It may refer to either mathematics or any of the other special sciences. In order that first philosophy be opposed to physics as second philosophy, the object of first philosophy must in some way or other precede the object of physics. In this respect, it would be more consistent to regard first philosophy as theology rather than to regard it as ontology. Actually the term δευτέρα

universal science above and beyond first philosophy. Aristotle himself was conscious of this problem and raised the question whether φιλοσοφία was a universal science or a science concerning a certain genus of being. This question was answered as follows. Just as among the mathematical sciences geometry and astronomy treat only of special things while general mathematics is applicable to everything, so the science of immovable substances is prior to physics and is first philosophy. Being first, it is also universal. This science deals with being *qua* being, what it is, and what belongs to it *qua* being. This argument, however, seems to be somewhat forced. The science of being *qua* being, i.e. ontology, was an inquiry into being, not in particular, but in general. Whereas the division of philosophy into physics, mathematics, and theology was a division by kinds of substance. I suspect that it is not consistent to make philosophy, on the one hand, a science of being *qua* being, and on the other hand to divide it according to its objects. In the one case, philosophy is distinguished from the special sciences in that it is a universal science. In the other case it is equivalent to theoretical knowledge in general which contains theology as a part. Thus philosophy as a universal science is confused with philosophy as a genus, and further a species belonging to this genus is confused with that universal science, the concept of first philosophy mediating between ontology and theology. Aristotle argues that, since immovable being is the first, the philosophy which deals with this kind of being is first philosophy, and since the science and its object are the first, they are also universal, so that this science is the same as ontology which deals with being *qua* being. Even if we admit that immovable and independent being is first in respect of value, it does not follow necessarily that the science of this object is universal, for there is no necessary relation between the most precious and the most universal.

Even if the order meant here was not the order of value, but the order of existence, knowledge of the most completely existent would

φιλοσοφία appears only once in *Met.* Z. 11. 1037a15, and this part is regarded by Jaeger as an interpolation. On the other hand, πρώτη φιλοσοφία appears beside the quoted passage in *Met.*, in *Phys.* I. 9. 192 a 36, II. 2. 194 b 14, and *De Cael.* I. 8. 277 b 10. In these places, however, what is called first philosophy is an enquiry into separate being or formal principles, and seems to be theology rather than ontology. In *Rep.* 379 A, Plato used θεολογία in the sense of 'theology.' But in Aristotle the word appears only twice, in *Met.* E.1. 1026 a 19 and *Met.* K. 7. 1046 b 3. What is called θεολογία or θεολογός in other places means in fact 'early cosmology' or 'cosmologist.' (cf. Ross' *Comm.* on 1026 a 19). In short, 'first philosophy' is a term suitable to theology rather than to ontology. For metaphysics as ontology, the term πρώτη ἐπιστήμη is more suitable. Metaphysics is the first science, insofar as it deals with substance as the primary being but it is the first philosophy, insofar as it deals with the first substance – not in the sense of the individual, but in the sense of God. But this distinction was not made clearly enough by Aristotle.

not be any the more knowledge of everything. The science of immovable and independent being may be the highest science, but is not necessarily the broadest. Theology is not first philosophy in the same sense as ontology is. Theology is first in the sense that it is concerned with the highest being, i.e. with God, while ontology is first in the sense that it is the broadest science and deals with everything. It might be thought a fault in Aristotle to have overlooked this difference. But rather than being an oversight it was natural and essential, if not necessary, to his system. In Aristotle, scientific knowledge was the inquiry into the principles and causes of being. There are four kinds of causes, viz., *causa finalis*, *causa formalis*, *causa efficiens*, and *causa materialis*. Of these four kinds of causes, the first rules the others as final principle. Consequently, the ideal of scientific knowledge, which explains being from its principles, was to explain everything with reference to the highest *causa finalis*. Since this highest cause is God, as pure separate form without matter, to relate everything to God was considered to be the ideal of complete explanatory knowledge. Thus it was a quite natural consequence of Aristotle's teleology that theology came to be identified with the first philosophy and ontology.

In short, according to Aristotle, metaphysics was, in the first place, first philosophy and the science of being *qua* being. It was also the science of substance, especially of the first substance, which is immovable, eternal, independent, and without matter, i.e. God. Thus first philosophy or ontology was at the same time theology. [1] The distinction between ontology and theology only remained implicit. These two branches of metaphysics which were separated by later philosophers were in Aristotle inextricably united.

---

[1] In *Metaphysics* only Γ is concerned with independent and immovable being. Therefore, if theology forms the main part of metaphysics, the other Books must be regarded as subordinate to this most essential part. Now, if it was an independent treatise outside the 10 vols. in the *Anonymus Menagii* list, most parts of Aristotle's *Metaphysics* must be assumed to have mere subordinate significance, either as a foundation of physics or as a theory of science. Only when we define metaphysics as the science of being *qua* being, or the science of substance in general, will these Books form the main parts of metaphysics, and theology by contrast become a special branch.

CHAPTER II

THE TRADITION OF THE CONCEPT
OF METAPHYSICS

I. ANCIENT INTERPRETATIONS

Metaphysics was defined by Aristotle in three different ways, firstly as the science which deals with being as being, secondly, as the science of immovable substance without matter, i.e. of God, thirdly, as the science of first principles. [1] Of these three definitions, the last mentioned gives the essence of science rather than of metaphysics. [2] The first and second definitions are both concerned with metaphysics in the proper sense, but there is a remarkable difference between them. This difference was taken seriously by Natorp [3] and it also became the basis of Jaeger's [4] theory which postulated a development of Aristotle's thought during his lifetime. The question of the validity of Jaeger's theory may be dismissed for the moment. We may accept, if necessary, Jaeger's view, and assume that the theological definition represents the thought of Aristotle's early period, when he was under Plato's influence, while the ontological definition represents his later thought. Even with this assumption we cannot suppose that he simply changed his view of metaphysics. For, as we have already said, Aristotle himself argued that these two definitions were in conformity with each other, for both defined the first science. We found that his argument was fallacious, as it turned on an ambiguity in the term 'the first,' but that it was none the less completely in accordance with his teleological system. We must notice, moreover, that the science of being *qua* being did not mean, as we are apt to think, the science of being as an abstract predicate or as a vague genus. According to Aristotle, being was not a genus, but an analogical universal. [5] The categories such as quality, quantity, relation, etc., were not species under a genus, but the *summa genera*, which were analogically linked together by the main category, substance. The unification of being consisted in this analogy between

---

[1] J. Owens, *The Doctrine of Being in the Aristotelian Metaphysics*, 1951, p. 5.
[2] *Met.* E. 1. 1025b6. K7. 1063b36. M2. 1076b36. Γ.2. 1003b16. *An. Post.* I. 13. 78a25.
[3] Natorp, 'Thema und Disposition der aristotelischen Metaphysik.' (*Philos. Monatschr.* XXIV [1888] 37–65; 540–574).
[4] Jaeger, *Aristoteles: Grundlegung einer Geschichte seiner Entwicklung*, 1923. *Studien zur Entstehungsgeschichte der Metaphysik des Aristoteles.* 1912.
[5] Cf. Owens, *op. cit.*, p. 9.

summa genera. Just for this reason, to explain being *qua* being was considered by Aristotle to be the same as to explain being with reference to substance. In other words, being was for Aristotle primarily a subject, and it was a predicate only in a secondary sense. Generally speaking, nominalism is a dominant current in modern times. It is on account of this modern dogma that the identification of universality with value appears to be strange. But Aristotle's explanation of the coincidence of the ontological and the theological definitions of metaphysics seems to have given his school no trouble.

It is not certain how Theophrastus [1] regarded the science of being *qua* being. But we know that both he and Alexander of Aphrodisias [2] considered that the science of first principles was the same as the science of divine being. According to Alexander, first philosophy coincides with theology. This science deals with the first causes of all being, and is therefore universal. Being is not an abstract general predicate, but the universal existence which forms the centre of all relations [3] and the cause of everything. Either being *qua* being is identical with immovable and independent existence, or at least ontology coincides with theology. This interpretation became the orthodox tradition from Syrianus and Asclepius to Eustratius and Clement of Alexandria. [4]

It is not certain when the difficulty of identifying the ontological definition with the theological was first noticed. But we may safely guess it to be earlier than Al-Farabi, for Avicenna gave an ingenious solution to this problem and the same idea appears though in a somewhat incomplete form in Al-Farabi. However, before considering the Arabian philosophers, we must look into the position which metaphysics occupied in ancient and mediaeval classifications. Needless to say, it was only with Plato and Aristotle that philosophy or science in general became the object of philosophical inquiry. Hence later writers model the classification of science or the theory of science upon these two great philosophers. Sextus Empiricus says that the tripartite classification of philosophy into Physics, Ethics, and Logic, which was attributed to Plato by Cicero, [5] originated with Xenocrates, and

---

[1] Theophrastus, *Metaph.* I. 1–4. Tr. Ross and Fobes, pp. 2–4 (Owens, p. 7).

[2] Alexander Aph. *In Met.* 245. 29–126,13. (Owens, p. 8).

[3] Alexander Aph., *op. cit.*, 447. 22–32. This part is generally considered to be a later supplement. But the thought is derived from Alexander. (Owen p. 9).

[4] Syrianus, *In Met.*, p. 55. 3–16, p. 58. 12–15; Asclepius, *In Met.*, p. 1. 17–20. 235. 33–236. 1. 225. 14–226. 25. 364. 22–25. 235. 12–13. 232. 4–11; Eustratius, *In Eth. Nic.*, p. 42. 10–12 etc. (Owens, p. 10f.).

[5] Cicero, *Acad. Post.* I. 5, 19.

was taken over by the Stoics. Of these three parts, the Stoics attached the greatest importance to ethics and regarded logic as a mere method. This Platonic type of classifications was adopted by Epicurus, [1] Cicero, [2] Seneca, Apuleius, Galen, and Philo Judaeus; then by the early Fathers [3] and by St. Augustine, [4] who was followed by Cassiodorus, Isidore, Scotus Eriugena, and Albertus Magnus. [5]

On the other hand, the Aristotelian classification divided science or philosophy firstly into the theoretical and practical parts, and then subdivided the former into Physics, Mathematics and Metaphysics (Theology), and the latter into Ethics, Economics and Politics. Strictly speaking this classification is due to Aristotle's followers, who accomplished it in conformity with Aristotle's thought. No important modification was made to this classification except that the question was brought forward by the Stoics whether logic was involved in the system of philosophy or was merely a preliminary to philosophy, and a subdivision of practical philosophy. [6] This type of classification was passed down through Andronicus, Alexander of Aphrodisias, Ammonius, Olympiodorus, Johannes Philoponus, Elias etc., [7] and became the orthodox view of the Scholastics who took it from the Arabian philosophers.

Compared with that of Plato, Aristotle's classification was much more detailed, and we must note carefully how metaphysics or theology became the main part of philosophy. Metaphysics was called either theology or first philosphy – these names being used as synonyms without any consideration either of the distinction between them, or of their relationship to each other.

Although metaphysical speculation died down after Aristotle, theory of science made progress in the Alexandrian school [8] which occupied itself interpreting and arranging the systems of its predecessors. Albinus [9] of Smyrna was a Platonist of the middle of the second

[1] Sextus Emp., *Adv. Math.* VII, 16.

[2] Cicero, *De Fin.* I. 19. 63; *De Or.* I. 15; Seneca, *Epist.* 8, 9, 11; Apuleius, Galen, *Hist. Phil.*, 6 (Diels, *Dox. Gr.* p. 603); Philo Jud., *de Agric.* (ed. Wendland) II. 92.

[3] Clemens Alex., *Strom.* IV, 26. *Philosophumena* Hippolyti; Hieronymus, *ad Paulam Urbicam*, ed. Erasm. IV, 90; Euseb., *Praep. Eu.* IX, 2. Joh. Lam. C. 68, C. 3; Isiodor, *Ep.* 11, 201; Lactant, *Diu.* III. 12ff.

[4] Augustinus, *Civitas Dei*, VIII, e. cf. II. 7. XI. 25. *Epist.* 3; 118, 3, 137, 5.

[5] L. Baur, *Dominicus Gundissalinus De Divisione Philosophiae*, Untersuchungen, 1903, II. p. 196.

[6] *Ibid.*, 197ff.

[7] Alexander Aph., *Com. In Met.*, ed. Hayduck, pp. 446, 658–661; Ammonius, *Ar.*, *Comm. Gr.* IV, 4; Simplicius (ed. Basil. 155), Olympiodorus (Littig, Andronikos Rod. 1. 49 ff.) Johannes Philoponus *In Cat. Arist.*, ed. Busse, *Ar. Comm.*, XVIII, I. p. 113ff. (Baur, p. 198).

[8] Baur, *op. cit.*, p. 325 ff.

[9] Albinus, λόγος διδασκαλικὸς τῶν Πλάτωνος δογμάτων; Dübner, *Platonis Opera*, III. p. 228 ff; Hermann, *Platonis Dial.*, VI. p. 152 ff. (Baur, p. 326).

century, but he adopted the Aristotelian type of classification and divided philosophy into the theoretical, the practical, and the dialectical. Theoretical philosophy was divided into Theology, Physics, and Mathematics; practical philosophy into Ethics, Economics, and Politics. Ammonius, [1] a representative of the Alexandrian school in the fifth century and a disciple of Proclus, also followed the Aristotelian classification and adopted the tripartite division. He was completely faithful to Aristotle especially with regard to the division of philosophy in accordance with the forms of being as subject matter. He divided theoretical science into three parts: theology corresponding to being without matter, physics corresponding to being accompanied by matter, and mathematics corresponding to being which in one sense was independent of matter and in another sense was accompanied by matter. He called metaphysics theology and postulated immaterial being as its object. This is, as is well known, the second definition of metaphysics given by Aristotle.

Due to its adoption by Ammonius, the Aristotelian type of classification became authoritative, and dominated all the Byzantine, Syrian, and Arabian philosophers. Among them the Arabian school has the greatest significance. Al-Kindi in the ninth century, Al-Farabi in the tenth, Avicenna and Al-Gasel in the eleventh, and Averroes in the twelfth made great contributions to the mediaeval world in transmitting Neo-Platonism and Aristotle's philosophy.

2. ARABIAN SCHOOL

Al-Farabi [2] divided his treatises on science into six parts: (1) *scientia linguae*, (2) *scientia logicae*, (3) *scientia doctrinalis*, (4) *scientia naturalis*, (5) *scientia civilis*, and (6) *scientia legum*. This division of science is, without doubt, dependent upon the Aristotelian type fixed by Ammonius. Grammar and logic, as the first and second, are preliminary parts, the third and the fourth parts involve mathematics, physics, and theology, which are all theoretical sciences. The fifth and the sixth parts are practical sciences, of which ethics and politics were regarded as the most important. Al-Farabi also called metaphysics [3] theology, but he dissented from the common prejudice that assumed the creator, reason,

---

[1] Ammonius, *Comm. In Isag. Porph.*, ed. Busse, p. 10 ff.; *Comm. In Cat.*, ed. Busse, p. 5 ff. (Baur, pp. 198, 230).

[2] Al-Farabi, *De Scientiis*, (Baur, p. 342).

[3] Al-Farabi, *Die Abhandlungen von den Tendenzen der Aristotelischen Metaphysik*, aus dem Arabischen übersetzt von Dieterici, 1892, p. 54 ff.

and mind to be the chief subjects of Aristotle's *Metaphysics*, pointing out that these subjects are only to be found in Met. Λ. He explained the identification of metaphysics with theology in the following way. He divided science into the general and the special. Special science, e.g. physics or mathematics, investigates special attributes of a particular being or idea, while universal or general science deals with the matters which are common to everything that exists, e.g. before and after, possibility, and actuality, completeness and incompleteness, as well as the principle common to all realities, i.e. God. Such a science must be unique, for, if there were two general sciences, each of them would have to have different objects, which would be paradoxical. Now, theology is a general science, for God as the object of this science is the principle of all absolute beings. Consequently, the science which studies the principle of reality must be theology. This science, being higher and more general than physics, comes after physics. Hence this science is called *meta*-physics.

We see how Al-Farabi was faithful to Aristotle's original idea in his definition of metaphysics, and in his identification of ontology and theology. The object of metaphysics is, according to him, firstly, absolute being and unity, which is equivalent in generality to absolute being; secondly, nothingness and the many, which are allotted to this science in accordance with the rule that opposites belong to the same science. Having fixed the main objects of metaphysics, he considers the species of these objects, which belong to metaphysics subordinately, e.g., the ten categories, the kinds of unity, the attributes of reality, such as are possible and actual, the complete and the incomplete, cause and effect, as well as the attributes of unity, such as essence, resemblance, equality, identity, parallelism, homogeneity, and finally the attributes of nothingness and the many. Next comes the investigation of the principles one by one and their application to the particular objects of special sciences. Thus general science is completed, and the principles and objects of the special sciences are made explicit. In Al-Farabi's explanation of the objects and contents of metaphysics, in his distinction of the primary and essential objects from the secondary and subordinate, we find an anticipation of the distinction between the subject-matter and the problem of metaphysics made by Avicenna and Averroes.

Avicenna's [1] contribution to the theory of science is more important

---

[1] Avicenna, *De Philosophia Prima*. Cf. C. Sauter, *Avicennas Bearbeitung der aristotelischen Metaphysik*, 1912. p. 44 ff. Baur, *op. cit.*, p. 346 ff.

than Al-Farabi's. He too followed Ammonius and divided philosophy into theoretical and practical parts: the former into physics, mathematics, and theology, the latter into ethics, economics and politics, and similarly with the more special branches. What stands out and deserves special attention is that Avicenna raised the question whether the object of metaphysics was being *qua* being or immovable substance without matter, i.e. God, or the causes of things. To this question he gives the following ingenious answer. He splits up what we generally call the object of science into *subjectum* and *id quod inquiritur*, [1] namely subject and problem. The *subjectum* of a science is in his view given as self-evident, [2] while that of which the existence is in question, or which has to be proved, is not a *subjectum*, but merely *id quod inquiritur*. The latter is only an 'accidental object' of metaphysics, while the former is a 'formal object.' Metaphysics is a science which deals with being as being, a science which inquires into the principle of being common to both immaterial and material beings. But insofar as God is the final goal of the inquiry into being *qua* being, the end of metaphysics, He is an important object of this science. Similarly with the four principles. The reality of these principles is what requires to be proved, so they cannot be the *subjectum* of metaphysics, i.e. as we would say, not the object of metaphysics in the proper sense. But, insofar as they are the principles of being, they may be the problems of the science which deals with being as being. This attempt to synthesize the ontological and theological definitions of metaphysics is an idea peculiar to Avicenna or at least cannot be found in Aristotle. Basing himself on this argument, Avicenna tries to classify metaphysics. In the first place, he says, it is the inquiry into the principles of being *qua* being, in the second place the inquiry into final principles, in the third place the inquiry into the attributes of things, and in the fourth place, finally, it is the inquiry into the principles of the sciences. The *id quod inquiritur* or the problems of metaphysics are, firstly, that which is independent of matter and its concomitant phenomena, secondly, that which is combined with matter only in such a relation as a cause is to its effects, thirdly, that which is partly combined with and partly separated from matter, which in any case, does not need matter in order to exist, and fourthly, material things seen from an immaterial aspect, such as movement and rest. In all these parts, philosophical inquiry is mainly concerned with conceptual essence which is not derived from matter.

[1] τὸ ζητούμενον cf. Sauter, *op. cit.*, p. 47, n.1.
[2] Arist., *An. Post.*, I. 1; *An. Post.*, I. 3; *Met.* A. 9; *Eth. Nic.*, VI. 6.

The reason why this science is called theology is, according to Avicenna, that it is superior to the other sciences. It yields superior knowledge and more complete proofs. It yields the knowledge of God and the causes that are derived from God. As for the name of metaphysics, Avicenna points out that this science is to be learned after the other sciences, especially after physics, and that the objects of this science are supernatural. The educational order of metaphysics and the supernatural character of its object are thus clearly recognised.

A hundred years later than Avicenna, in the second half of the twelfth century, Averroes' activity demands our attention. He wrote many commentaries on Aristotle's works, and, in opposition to Avicenna, he set out to purify Aristotle's thought from any Neoplatonic taint. Not being proficient in Greek, he had to rely on the Arabian texts. [1] In his theory of science, [2] he opposed theoretical science to practical, and, besides these, admitted logic as useful to both theoretical and practical sciences. Theoretical science is either general or special; the former investigates being in its absolute meaning, the latter studies its essential attributes. There are three kinds of general theoretical science: Dialectic, Sophistic and Metaphysics. Dialectic and Sophistic deal with logical being *qua* being, Metaphysics deals with reality *qua* being. Physics and Mathematics are the branches of special theoretical science. The one is concerned with changeable being, the other with quanta separate from matter. The three branches of theoretical science, physics, mathematics, and metaphysics correspond to three parts of reality. The one part is the things which are in matter, the second part is the things which are in matter, though matter does not form a part of their definition. As to the third group, Averroes, instead of calling it being without matter, states that in physics there are principles which exist neither in matter nor in a special state, but in a general form. These principles are to be investigated by a general science.

Further, there are some general notions which belong to things perceptible by sense as well as to things not perceptible by sense, e.g. one and many, possible and actual, and other general attributes. These attributes are derived from incorporeal things and attributed to sensible things. They are the objects of the science which deals with being in general. Theoretical science of reality therefore is divided into gener-

---

[1] Geyser, 'Mittelalterliche Philosophie' in *Lehrbuch der Philosophie*, ed. Dessoir, II. p. 286.
[2] Averroës, *Die Metaphysik des A. nach dem Arabischen*, übersetzt und erläutert von Max Horton, 1912, p. 1–9.

al and special parts. The special part consists of physics and mathematics, and the general part inquires into being *qua* being or species of being, moving from the general to the special until it reaches the objects of the special sciences. It also ascends to the essential attributes of being and the series of categories up to the first cause, viz., the separate substance. Among various causes, metaphysics gives us only knowledge of the formal and the final cause. In giving explanations of cause and effect, metaphysics takes into consideration God and the divine being. Such a divine being is not in matter. The essential aim of Aristotle's metaphysics was, according to Averroes, to gain knowledge of the highest cause of perceptible things. Physics could not give such knowledge, because it gave us the explanation of the material and efficient cause, but not of the formal or final cause. The knowledge of these causes was given by the science of universal things, so that it belonged to metaphysics. But so far as this kind of knowledge presupposes that the existence of the first mover which is not in matter but distinct from efficient cause is to be required by physics, it presupposes physics.

As is evident from the above explanation, by turning metaphysics into general theoretical science, Averroes subsumes immaterial being – which is surely a special object – under this same science. This idea is derived from Aristotle's theory which identifies ontology with theology.

To meet the difficulties involved in this identification Averroes adopts Avicenna's interpretation and distinguishes the end or the formal object of metaphysics from the parts or material objects of metaphysics. Being *qua* being is the end of metaphysics. The parts or material objects are firstly the existence of sensible things and the genera i.e., the ten categories and their attributes. Secondly the principle of substance, i.e., incorporeal being, what reality it has, and how it is related to God as the principle of being. This part also includes the properties and activities of God, the relation of things in the world to God, and both the individual and the common attributes of incorporeal substance. Thirdly, the postulates of the special sciences, though this is merely a supplement to metaphysics. What Averroes calls here the end or the formal object of metaphysics corresponds to Avicenna's subject of metaphysics and his part or material object corresponds to Avicenna's problem.

As for the advantages of metaphysics, Averroes maintains that theoretical knowledge perfects the mind with the knowledge which brings the possibility of mind into actuality. Metaphysics gives a special explanation of the highest causes of reality and brings the special sciences to completion. In the order of learning, it comes after physics, for metaphysics presupposes physics as a postulated principle. Hence it is called metaphysics. But in the order of being, it precedes the other sciences and is called the first philosophy.

As for the method of metaphysics, Averroes uses the inductive method, which leads us from what *we* know to what is to be known by nature. It starts either from what is self-evident, or from what is discovered by physics – a remarkable contrast to later metaphysics, which adopted analytical logic *a priori* as its method. We may look on this as an example of Arabian empiricism as well as a faithful interpretation of Aristotle's philosophy. Though Averroes was an opponent of Avicenna, we find no essential difference between them as far as the characterization of the object, problem, and name of metaphysics is concerned.

3. EARLY SCHOLASTICS

It was only in the twelfth century that Aristotle became known to European Christians through the Arabian philosophers. The concept of metaphysics was also introduced to the Scholastics by the Arabians. Before this Arabian influence, Boethius [1] was the traditional authority in European thought. He divided philosophy into the theoretical and the practical, and subdivided each of these into three in the usual Aristotelian way. To designate the object of metaphysics, he uses a new term *intellectibile*, which is self-identical and forms the attribute of God. The second object of metaphysics is *intelligibile*. This is an incorporeal intellectual being which is degraded through being combined with body. Psychology is the science which deals with this kind of being. There is some inconsistency in Boethius' theory, since he considers mathematics to be the second part of theoretical science. [2]

Cassiodorus [3] acknowledged only theology and the seven liberal arts, and neglected metaphysics, physics and ethics. By 'theology' he meant the Christian theology of revelation, which became the queen of sciences in place of metaphysics. Thus the trend of thought turned against the Greek tradition. But in the twelfth century, due to the

---

[1] Boethius, *In Porphyrius Isagoge*, cf. Baur, *op. cit.*, p. 351, n.2.
[2] Boethius, *De Trinitate* 2.
[3] Cassiodorus Senator, *Institutiones divinarum et saecularium litterarum* (Baur, p. 352 f.).

influence of Abelard, ethics came into fashion again, and at the same time in the Arabian school natural science was flourishing. As the works of Al-Kindi, Al-Farabi, Avicenna, Al-Gazel, and Averroes, along with their versions of Aristotle's works, became better known, so the Aristotelian classification prevailed.

Before Averroes, Dominicus Gundissalinus, basing himself on Arabic and Latin traditions, arrived at a new conception of philosophy. In opposition to the religious and theological tendency of the preceding period, he secularised philosophy, extending it to cover both theology and metaphysics. According to Gundissalinus, [1] philosophy is concerned with being, which either depends or does not depend on our acts. The philosophy which deals with the former is practical, having conduct as its end, and the philosophy which deals with the latter is theoretical, knowledge being its end. Amongst the things which are independent of our acts, there are both immovables, like God and the angels, and concepts applicable to things which move, such as same, single, cause and effect. But the latter are further divided into what cannot exist without movement, e.g. humanity or solid geometry, and what can exist without movement, e.g. single, cause and effect. At least in some cases things to which movement essentially belong are in knowledge separable from matter. But in other cases even this form of separation is not possible, e.g. in the case of humanity. Anything to which movement is not essential, but in fact is moving, can be observed in two ways, namely either by itself apart from matter, or from the point of view of movement. In short, there are three kinds of being independent of us: (1) that which either essentially does not involve movement, or that which can exist or is known without movement though does not reject movement absolutely; (2) that which actually moves, but can be known intellectually apart from movement; (3) that which from its essence and being involves movement and change. Corresponding to these three classes, there are three branches of theoretical science: theology, mathematics, and physics. Practical philosophy is on the other hand divided into politics, economics, and ethics. Among theoretical sciences theology or the first philosophy is the highest. It is based upon the results of physics and mathematics, and aims at knowing the order of the world governed by God and the angels. Theology is, according to Gundissalinus, a science of independent being, and consequently is the most certain and the first. It is to be called *sapientia* rather than *scientia*. As *sapientia*, it is concerned with the most universal objects,

---

[1] Gundissalinus, *op. cit.*, Prologus, pp. 3–19; Baur, *Unters.*, pp. 186–193.

itself most certain and universal, the science of the first cause. Being
such a science, theology is superior to any other 'theoria,' and must
inquire into the principles of physics and mathematics, for everything
is the result of God, who is the cause of causes, the principle of principles. [1]

Gundissalinus' distinction of *scientia* and *sapientia* is evidently due
to Aristotle's distinction of ἐπιστήμη and σοφία. The three characteristics of *sapientia* also come from Aristotle's theory. They are namely
universality of objects, universality of knowledge, and knowledge of
principles. [2]

As to the *aporia* of the objects of metaphysics, he follows Avicenna
in distinguishing the subject from the problem – which he calls *materia*
– of theology (metaphysics). Gundissalinus rejects the popular opinion,
according to which the four causes or God are the subjects of theology,
on the grounds that it is misleading. For it is Aristotle's fundamental
rule that no science can prove the existence of its subject; the proof
must be given by a higher science. But in theology we meet questions
about God and causes, so that they cannot be the subject of this
science. The subject of theology, therefore, must be the most self-
evident concept, namely 'being.' Since theology is the highest science,
having no higher science above it, this highest and universal concept
'being' must be its subject. [3]

Though the subject of theology is 'being' instead of God or indepen-
pendent things, this does not prevent our making God the problem of
this science. Thus, theology is divided, following Avicenna, into four
parts which correspond to four kinds of subject: (1) God and spirits,
which are both absolutely separate from matter, (2) things which are
combined with matter, but as its cause, (3) things which can be found
both in matter and in immaterial things, e.g. cause or unity, (4) material things such as motion and rest. [4]

According to Gundissalinus, the 'species' of theology are the following
four pairs of concepts; substance and attributes, general and special,
cause and effect, possible and actual, which he calls *consequentia entia*,
i.e. accidents of being; the stages of theology are, first to inquire into
essences, second to exhibit the principles of proof, third to exhibit the
principles of logic, mathematics, and physics, and lastly to instruct in
immaterial essence and its reality. Metaphysics regards this essence

[1] Gundissalinus. *op. cit.*, p. 35, Baur, p. 267.
[2] Cf. Ch. I, 2.
[3] Gundissalinus, *op. cit.*, p. 36; Baur, p. 268 f.
[4] *Ibid.*, p. 37.

as absolute unity and indicates it as unity, being, truth, and the first.
Since this essence is the same as God, metaphysics exhibits God's relationship to the world, the generation and existence of essences, their
stages and combination, God's action in them, and their harmony,
completeness, and goodness. In short, metaphysics is a science of being,
which Gundissalinus assumed to be essences. And, making these
essences relate to God as the final cause, he identified metaphysics
with theology. The three definitions of metaphysics, namely, a science
of "being *qua* being," "a science of God and spirits as immaterial beings"
and "a science of the final principle," were thus combined, following
the tradition of Aristotle and Avicenna.

Gundissalinus usually called this science *scientia divina*, but he sometimes used such names as *philosophia prima*, *metaphysica*, and *causa
causarum*. He called it *scientia divina*, because it was the most excellent
science which proved the existence of God, *philosophia prima*, because
it was the science of the first cause, *causa causarum*, because it dealt
with God as the cause of everything, *metaphysica*, because it came
after physics in the order of education. [1]

Though Gundissalinus' work mainly consisted in extracts from Al-
Farabi and Avicenna, and it is doubtful to what extent he was critical
in making his extracts, his attempts at the synthesis and analysis of
metaphysical concepts were fairly successful. Hence his work became
the archetype of later Scholastic theories and even the greatest Scholastics, Albertus and St. Thomas, were no exceptions.

4. MIDDLE SCHOLASTICS

Thomas Aquinas established his system under the general influence
of Gundissalinus, but was also directly influenced by Avicenna and
Averroes. [2] He divided philosophy into the real and the rational. The
former is divided into speculative (theoretical) and practical (moral).
Theoretical philosophy includes physics, mathematics, and theology;
practical philosophy includes ethics, economics, and politics. Rational
philosophy or logic is not only a method, but also a part of philosophy. It
is however independent of the other branches. Theoretical philosophy
seeks knowledge for its own sake, while practical philosophy is concerned with conduct. Physics deals with the qualitative relations of

[1] *Ibid.*, p. 38.
[2] Thomas Aquinas, *Opuscula*, 70, qu. 5; *De Veritate*, qu. 14. cf. Werner, *Der heilige Thomas von Aquino*, 1859, II, pp. 147–166.

things which have sensible matter, mathematics with the quantitative relations of things accompanied by intelligible matter. And metaphysics deals with immaterial objects such as the possible and the actual, the one and the many, God and the angels, etc. The same science is called from different points of view either metaphysics, or first philosophy, or theology. [1] There are two kinds of theology; the one is philosophical, the other depends upon revelation. The objects of physics are the nature of movable things and their intellectual causes; the objects of mathematics are the things which, though movable and material, are independent of matter and movement. The object of theology is quite independent of movement and matter. This object is the most real and the highest principle of all other things. Insofar as it is the ultimate ground of all reality, it belongs to philosophical theology, but insofar as it is the highest reality, it belongs to positive theology. [2] In respect of method, physics is *rationaliter*, mathematics is *demonstraliter*, and theology is *intellectualiter*. The 'rational faculty' or the faculty of Understanding which is used in physics starts from sensible observation and moves one thing to another. The method of mathematics is (demonstrative or) discursive; it does not move from one thing to another, but moves rather from one determination to another determination of the same object, presupposing a single definition which combines these particular determinations. Only first philosophy (or theology) which employs the intellectual method, leads us through logic alone to a definite and certain conclusion. [3]

'Rational' cognition is concerned with the many, peripheral, and temporal beings, while 'intellectual' cognition refers to unique, central and eternal being. Since theology is a science which deals with the highest reality and the principles of being, intellectual intuition is most suitable to this science. [4] The name 'metaphysics' or 'first philosophy' is closely connected with its intellectual method. The reason why theology is called metaphysics or transphysics is that it has to be studied after physics. The rational thinking of the other sciences depends on the knowledge of theology. This determination is done in two ways. The one is to regress from effect to cause until one reaches the final cause, which is an independent substance and belongs to metaphysics. The other is to ascend from what is special to what is universal and reach 'being,' which is the most universal concept and of course

---

[1] Thomas Aquinas, *Opusc.* 70, qu. 5. Art. 1.
[2] *Ibid.*, qu. 5. Art. 4.
[3] *Ibid.*, qu. 7. Art. 1.
[4] *Ibid.*

the object of metaphysics. Further, theology is called 'first philosophy' because it deals with the principles which synthetically explain everything that is involved in the special science. [1] We see how St. Thomas was faithful to tradition in thus adopting all three determinations of Aristotle's metaphysics; namely, ontology, theology, and the theory of principles.

In another place, St. Thomas says that the subject of metaphysics is common being, though metaphysics also deals with the first cause and independent being. One might possibly take this to be an emphasis on the ontological aspect of metaphysics. [2] Still it is neither the same as Albertus Magnus' [3] opinion that the theological aspect was Plato's theory and not Aristotle's, nor is it the same as Duns Scotus' [4] opinion that the ontological definition is to be preferred to the theological, the former being derived from Avicenna and the latter from Averroes. St. Thomas' real intention becomes clearer from the context in which his remarks are made. In the preface to the commentary on Aristotle's metaphysics, [5] where they are to be found, he says *sapientia*, a science that rules other sciences and arts, is concerned with *maxime intelligibilia*. This most intelligible being may be interpreted in three ways. Firstly, with respect to the order of knowledge, the knowledge of causes is the most intelligible and the science of the first cause is supreme. Secondly, comparing intellect with sense, intellect is concerned with the universal, and sense with the particular. So the science which deals with the most universal is the most intellectual. These universal principles are, e.g., being and what belongs to being, the one and the many, possibility and actuality, etc. Thirdly, from the point of view of intellectual knowledge itself, that which is most distant from matter is the most intellectual, especially what is separate from matter not only in intellect, but also in existence, namely God or *intelligentiae*.

According to St. Thomas, these three points of view are in the final issue reduced to one, and the three objects, viz., separate substance, universal being, and the first cause are reduced to one single science. Separate substance is universal and essentially the first cause. Seeing that the cause proper to each genus is to be investigated by the science which deals with the genus itself, separate substance and common

[1] *Ibid.*
[2] Owens, *op. cit.*, p. 5.
[3] Albertus Magnus, *Met.* I. I. 2. op. VI. 6b; Owens, p. 5.
[4] Duns Scotus, *Quest. Metaph.* I. 1. op. VII. 11–37.
[5] Thomas Aquinas, *In Met. Prooemium.*

being, i.e. the genus, must belong to the same science, for separate sub-stance is the cause of genus.

After this comes a statement of the view we have already considered: "Though this science considers these three, it does not investigate any one of them as its subject. The subject is rather common being. We study its cause or modus, and not the cause of any genus we like. For the knowledge of the cause of any genus we like is the end of scientific investigation (rather than its subject). And even if the subject of this science is common being, it may be concerned with what is separate from matter both in existence and in intellect. For what is thought to be separate from matter both in existence and in intellect is not con-fined to what cannot be in matter, i.e. God or intelligible substance, but may also be what can be without matter, viz. common being. This would not be the case if something were dependent on matter for its existence."

Careful reading shows that St.Thomas does not here go so far as to refuse metaphysics the cognition of separate substance which is in-dependent of matter, and of principles. He only means to say that separate substance and principles are the problems of metaphysics and not its subject. This is, as we have seen before, a thesis maintained by Avicenna and Gundissalinus. What is peculiar to St. Thomas' argument about the object of metaphysics is, in the first place, that he calls 'being *qua* being' 'common being' or 'genus'; in the second place, that he makes immaterial substance the common cause of being; and in the third place, that he assumes two kinds of separate being, firstly, separate substance in the primary sense, which cannot exist in matter, and secondly, another being which can be without matter; common being belongs to this immaterial thing in the secondary sense.

These interpretations of metaphysics raise some important problems for us. Provided that being *qua* being is the same as common being, the science which deals with this object is what will later be called *meta-physica generalis*. But when independent substance is the problem, if not the subject, of metaphysics, it is what will later be called *meta-physica specialis;* though the distinction between these two terms is not made before Wolff. Instead of making this distinction, St. Thomas put forward the second interpretation, according to which independent substance is the cause of all things. If this cause should be taken as *causa finalis*, this idea is not discordant with Aristotle's teleological thought. But, in fact, St. Thomas regards it as *causa efficiens*, and moreover his reference to Aristotle does not seem to support his argument. [1]

The third idea, which assumes common being as a kind of immaterial being, was taken up by Suarez. This is a fallacious distribution of Aristotle's term 'separate in existence,' and makes its distinction from 'separate in intellect,' which is an attribute of mathematical object, obscure. Taking this difficulty into consideration, later Scholastics divided metaphysics into *metaphysica generalis* and *metaphysica specialis*. In short, St. Thomas' view of metaphysics, with its various new ideas, on the whole remained faithful to the tradition from Al-Farabi, Avicenna, and Gundissalinus.

5. LATER SCHOLASTICS

Francis Suarez, a Spanish Scholastic of the sixteenth century, followed tradition in finding the *objectum potissimum*, [2] i.e. adequate object, in God, immaterial substance, substance in general, and real attributes. [3] To inquire into these objects is taken by him to be the same as to inquire into being as being. According to Suarez, God is evidently the object of metaphysics as it was dealt with in Aristotle's Met. Λ. That Aristotle called this science theology, [4] first philosophy, [5] or the ruler of the sciences, [6] was due to his reverence for this object. Metaphysics is also called divine because it inquires into the first cause. It is thought to be superior to physics, because it studies the universal and the first substance. All these characterizations prove that God is the object of metaphysics. [7] Suarez however is not of the same opinion as those who take God to be the only object of metaphysics. Sua-

---

[1] This interpretation appears not only in the preface to the commentary on Aristotle's *Metaphysics* but also more minutely in the *Comm. 1164*, which is related to *Met.* E. 1. 1026a17. St. Thomas, according to the Latin text he used read: "Necesse vero communes quidem causas sempiternas, et maxime has: *hae* namque causae manifestis sensibilium sunt." Thus he understood the immaterial and unmovable body to be the cause of sensible things. But the original text is not ταῦτα γὰρ αἴτια τοῖς φανεροῖς τῶν αἰσθητῶν (J γρ. E γρ. Al) but ταῦτα γὰρ αἴτια τοῖς φανεροῖς τῶν θείων. This must be translated 'haec etenim causae manifestis divinorum sunt.' It is not the cause of sensible things, but the cause of manifest divine being; St. Thomas' interpretation is misleading.

[2] *Objectum potissimum* (adequate object) meant at that time the object which completely corresponded to the whole capacity of cognition or the realm of fundamental objects, on which the various branches of science were concentrated. Cf. E. Conze, *Der Begriff der Metaphysik bei Franziskus Suarez*, 1928, pp. 5–7.

[3] Suarez, *Disputationes Metaphysicae* I. 1.34; Conze, p. 8.

[4] *Met.* A. 2. 983b5–10. K. 6. 1064b3; Suarez I, 1.17; Conze, p. 9.

[5] *Met.* I. 1004a4.Δ. 1026a23 ff; Suarez. I. C.1, 1, 15. I. 2, 4, *et passim*; Conze, p. 9.

[6] *Met.* 996b10–13. Suarez, I. B.

[7] *Met.* 1005a31–b1. Suarez, I. 17. I, 1, 17.

rez, following tradition, wrongly attributes this opinion to Al-Farabi, but in fact Al-Farabi's opinion was, as we have seen above, more consistent. At any rate, Suarez was opposed to this interpretation, not only because of his Christian view that human nature is finite and cannot comprehend God directly, but also because Aristotle himself dealt in his metaphysics with many problems other than God. [1] According to Suarez, Aristotle admitted not only the object of physics, but also superior substances which are immaterial and are the objects of metaphysics. This science was afterwards called metaphysics, meaning *transphysica*, a science which was concerned with the objects lying beyond physical things. [2]

The theory which admits only immaterial substance to be the object of metaphysics is commonly believed to be Avicenna's. [3] Suarez both points out the incorrectness of this attribution, and rejects the theory itself. He considers that metaphysics must treat of objective concepts common both to material and immaterial substances, since they are related to each other. [4] Aristotle in fact treats of material substances with their principles, matter and form, in Met. H and θ. Seen from a systematic point of view, immaterial substance must correspond to material substance, since one is the privation of the other. [5]

Further, the object of metaphysics must include not only substance, but also its real attributes. 'Being' is a concept which includes both substances and their attributes. Metaphysics is the first of all sciences, and must treat the first or the most universal thing, which is precisely being *qua* being. [6] Aristotle, Avicenna, St. Thomas and Albertus Magnus were all of the same opinion. [7] Thus Suarez, by taking being *qua* being to be the same as the universal and the first, made it include immaterial substances as well as other objects. Along with the definition 'the science of being *qua* being,' Suarez considered another characterization of no less importance, namely, 'the science which deals with being, viewed abstracted from matter in its existence.' [8] This idea was in Aristotle's metaphysics, and from it was derived the division of the three theoretical sciences, viz. physics, mathematics, and

[1] Suarez, I. 1,10; Conze, p. 10.
[2] Suarez, I. B.
[3] This theory is attributed in fact to Nicolaus Cusanus' disciple, Bovillus (ca. 1510). cf. Stöckl, *Gesch. d. Phil. d. Mittelalters*, III, p. 88; Conze, p. 22.
[4] Suarez, I. 1,13.
[5] *Ibid.*, I. 2,5.
[6] *Ibid.*, I. 1,21.
[7] *Ibid.*, I. 1,24.
[8] *Ibid.*, I. 3,1.

metaphysics. The object of physics is sensible matter, the object of mathematics intelligible matter. The one is movable while the other is immovable. The object of mathematics is separable from matter only in thought, but in existence it is accompanied by material substance. But the object of metaphysics is separate from matter both in knowledge and in existence. So far, Suarez is faithful to Aristotle. But, following St. Thomas, he identifies metaphysics as a science which deals with the object separate from matter in existence, with metaphysics as a science which deals with being *qua* being. [1]

To reconcile the two different definitions of metaphysics, the one as the science of being *qua* being, the other as the science of independent, immovable, and immaterial substance, Suarez distinguishes two meanings of the expression "separate from matter in existence." In one sense it means "never existing in matter," in another sense it means, as St. Thomas said, [2] "sometimes not in matter, sometimes combined with matter, in any case matter not belonging to its concept," in other words, 'indifferent as to whether it is material or immaterial'; as are, for example, being, one, good, substance, attribute, and created. [3] Cause is also a concept common to both material and immaterial beings; it may be the object of metaphysics.

In short, according to Suarez, concepts of material objects, in abstraction from matter, are objects for the science of being *qua* being, as are purely immaterial beings. This idea, ingenious as it is, and also to be found in St. Thomas, obscures (as we have already said) the distinction between immaterial being in the secondary sense and the mathematical object which is abstracted from matter in thought. To avoid this difficulty, later Scholastics tried to divide metaphysics into general and special parts, allotting ontology to the former, and theology to the latter. [4] This new interpretation gradually came to dominate not only the Protestant Scholastics, but also the Catholic school. It was in Christian Wolff that this idea became most explicit. In Wolff, *metaphysica generalis* is ontology or first philosophy, while *metaphysica specialis* includes cosmology and psychology as well as natural theology.

---

[1] *Ibid.*, I. 3,1. cf. Conze, pp. 16–18.
[2] Thomas Aqu. proe. *In Met.* fin. Avicenna, *In Met.* I. 5a2. n.; Boethius, *De Trini.* 2, 1, a 4, Conze, p. 19.
[3] Suarez, I, 1,13.
[4] Conze, p. 65. Cf. E. Weber, *Die philosophische Scholastik des protestantischen Deutschlands*, p. 91 ff

6. WOLFFIAN SCHOOL

According to Wolff, philosophy, in distinction from history and mathematics, is characterized as rational knowledge of being or possible meaning. He also defines philosophy as a science which inquires into possible being, as far as it is possible. [1] What is most remarkable is the emphasis on possibility, an entirely new idea, though characteristic of the so-called Continental Rationalism, which attaches importance to logical or ideal form as compared with reality, along with its determination of the method of philosophy as rational.

Now philosophy is divided into three parts: natural theology, psychology, and physics, each with a corresponding object; God, the human mind, and body respectively. [2] Natural theology is a science of possibilities to do with God, [3] psychology is a science of possibilities to do with the human mind, [4] and physics is a science of possibilities to do with body. [5]

Mind aims at the knowledge of truth and desires what is good. Logic and practical philosophy correspond to these faculties. Logic is useful to the faculty of knowing the truth, and practical philosophy is useful to the faculty of desiring the good. Practical philosophy is divided into ethics, politics, economics, and natural law – the last mentioned being a supplement to the three traditional branches. The science which sums up the branches of practical philosophy is called general practical philosophy. Liberal arts, such as technics, grammar, rhetoric, or poetics may be called philosophy insofar as these arts take on a scientific form. [6]

Now, there is a being common to all beings. This is common to mind and body, to natural things and the products of art. The science which is concerned with this common being is called *ontologia* or *philosophia prima*. [7] Body is considered either in its general aspects or in special aspects. So that physics is divided into general physics and special physics. [8] The science which deals with bodies in the world as a whole is cosmology. It is also divided into general cosmology and special cosmology. [9] Psychology and physics are sometimes given the general

---

[1] Wolff, *Logica*, I. para. 6, cf. para. 17.
[2] *Ibid.*, III. para. 55, 56.
[3] *Ibid.*, para. 57.
[4] *Ibid.*, para. 58.
[5] *Ibid.*, para. 59.
[6] *Ibid.*, para. 61 and 72.
[7] *Ibid.*, para. 73.
[8] *Ibid.*, para 75 and 76.
[9] *Ibid.*, para. 77 and 78.

name of *pneumatica*. [1] Ontology, general cosmology, and *pneumatica* are subdivisions of *metaphysica*. [2] Thus in Wolff's philosophy *metaphysica* became a synthetic science which dealt with being, world, and mind. [3] As for the order of these philosophical sciences, logic comes first in accordance with the rule that the part which involves the principle of others is prior. On this same ground metaphysics precedes physics. Among metaphysical sciences, ontology comes first, then general cosmology and psychology, and lastly natural theology. [4]

We suggested that in later Scholastics the idea of dividing metaphysics into the general and the special already existed in embryo. But it was Wolff who first developed it. Being *qua* being, which was called by Avicenna the subject of metaphysics, became the object of *metaphysica generalis*, or of *ontologia*. God, mind, and principles, Avicenna's problems, became the object of *metaphysica specialis*. The term *ontologia* first appeared in Gocleneus' *Lexicon Philosophicum* [5]. Clauberg, [6] a Cartesian, used it synonymously with *ontosophia*, and Wolff adopted it to express the content of *metaphysica generalis*, and identified it with first philosophy. The division of *metaphysica specialis* into cosmology, psychology, and natural science is also due to Wolff. Before him, physics and psychology had been excluded in later Scholastics from metaphysics and were considered as branches of theoretical science. But once *metaphysica* was divided into the general and the special, it could no longer be described as an absolutely general science, and *metaphysica specialis* also had to be subdivided into several branches. As we have said, there already was a view according to which mind or even principles of material substances were objects of metaphysics along with God as an immaterial, independent, and immovable substance. In most cases, however, these objects were reduced either to being as being or to God as the first principle.

It was Wolff's original idea to set up special branches of metaphysics distinguished from empirical researches. The traditional problem of whether metaphysics was the science of being *qua* being or the science of immaterial substance admittedly found a clear cut solution in Wolff. But this solution must be regarded as Wolff's own theory rather than as his interpretation of Aristotle's metaphysics. At least

---

[1] *Ibid.*, para. 79.
[2] *Ibid.*
[3] *Ibid.*
[4] *Ibid.*, para. 99.
[5] Gocleneus, *Lexicon Philosoph.* 1613, p. 16.
[6] Clauberg, *Opera*, p. 281.

we must not overlook the clear difference between the two thinkers' conceptions of being and generality. In Wolff, being is no longer a universal principle at the centre of various relations. It is nothing more than an abstract general concept. Metaphysics becomes a system of pure conceptual knowledge, without any trace of empirical influence.

According to Wolff, general cosmology treats what is common to both the actual and the possible worlds. He proudly declares [1] that he originated this science by making the question which had previously only occasionally been posed into an independent inquiry. He is also proud of his distinction [2] between rational and empirical psychology, though rational psychology itself, he admits, was not originated by him. In all likelihood, the idea of including psychology in metaphysics had its supporters in much earlier times. [3] Toletus, the teacher of Suarez, in his psychology, [4] gives us two theories based on this idea, without however mentioning the names of their supporters. The one theory maintains that mind and body are to be investigated by physics insofar as they are combined, but are to be studied by metaphysics insofar as they exist independently of each other. The other theory maintains that physicists study the sensible and vegetable mind, while metaphysicians deal with the rational and intellectual mind. Suarez, [5] with Toletus, opposed these theories, maintaining that mind is the object of physics since it is essentially combined with body and is defined in terms of matter and body. But for the fact that Aristotle treated psychology in a separate book from his *Metaphysics*, such an idea might never have come to be held, as the converse seems to be more inherently plausible. It is generally admitted nowadays that Aristotle in his later period considered mind to be the form of body and used the notion of body in defining mind. In this respect Suarez' interpretation proves valid. However, not only in his youth, but throughout his life, Aristotle held that at least a part of mind was separate from matter. The Christian Scholastics would much prefer to make minds and angels approach to God and make them the objects of metaphysics rather than leaving them in nature. This is just the direction in which Wolff advanced, except that he did not believe in the existence of angels and did not find it necessary to distinguish between minds and

---

[1] Wolff, *op. cit.*, III, para. 78.
[2] *Ibid.*, para 112, and 111.
[3] Conze, *op. cit.*, p. 68.
[4] Toletus, *De Anima*, q. 2. prooem. Conze, p. 67.
[5] Suarez, *op. cit.*, I, 2, 19 and 20; Conze, p. 68.

angels. Thus God and the human mind were finally taken to be the objects of *pneumatica*. [1]

Wolff's classification of the sciences, especially his theory of metaphysics, was taken over by his disciple Alexander Baumgarten, who defined metaphysics as the science of the grounds of human knowledge.[2] Metaphysics thus tended to become the theory of knowledge, a tendency which was, of course, already present in Wolff. Thus Wolff made possible being the object of metaphysics; he put the sciences in an order depending on the sources of their principles. Making logic precede metaphysics, he emphasized rationality within metaphysics. Baumgarten went even further in these directions. Like Wolff, he divided metaphysics into ontology, cosmology, psychology, and natural theology. [3] He called ontology by many other names: *ontosophia*, *metaphysica*, *metaphysica universalis*, *architectonica*, *philosophia prima* etc., and maintained that it was the science of general or abstract predicates of things. [4] Ontology belonged to *metaphysica* because general predicates belonged to the first ground of human knowledge. [5] The concept of being was taken logically as a general predicate. To define ontology as a science of abstract predicates ran counter to Aristotle's original idea, which emphasised the subject-character of being. Metaphysics gradually inclined towards logic or the rationalistic theory of knowledge. The predicates with which ontology was concerned were divided into inner and outer, and the inner were further divided into what belonged to things in common and what belonged to them alternatively. [6] *Cosmologia generalis* is the science of the various genera of the world. When knowledge is derived from experience it is *cosmologia empirica*, and when it is deduced from our abstract concept of the world it is *cosmologia rationalis*. [7] Since cosmology involves the fundamental laws of psychology, physics, theology, and practical wisdom, it belongs to metaphysics. [8] The objects of cosmology are abstract concepts, the parts and the completeness of the world. [9]

Psychology is the science of abstract predicates of the soul. [10] Its propositions form *psychologia empirica*, which is based empirically on

[1] Wolff, *op. cit.*, para. 79.
[2] A. Baumgarten, *Metaphysik*, 1766, para. 1.
[3] *Ibid.*, para. 2.
[4] *Ibid.*, para. 4.
[5] *Ibid.*, para. 5.
[6] *Ibid.*, para. 6.
[7] *Ibid.*, para. 252.
[8] *Ibid.*, para. 253.
[9] *Ibid.*, para. 254.
[10] *Ibid.*, para. 367.

what is familiar to us, and *psychologia rationalis*, [1] which is deduced by means of very long chains of reasoning from the abstract concept of soul. Finally, natural theology is the science of God as far as He is knowable without faith. [2] It belongs to metaphysics because it involves the rudimentary principles of practical wisdom, teleology, and the theory of revelation. [3] The objects of natural theology are God and His work. [4]

Baumgarten's metaphysical theory is a development of Wolff's conceptualism. Metaphysics leaves behind its original meaning of the science of being, and becomes a science of knowledge. The branches of special metaphysics are attributed to metaphysics because they involve the foundations of other sciences. This is a remarkable characteristic of modern philosophy as opposed to ancient and mediaeval philosophy, which was mainly concerned with being and only treated of knowledge indirectly or derivatively. Baumgarten is inevitably the dominant influence on Kant's view of metaphysics, for Kant adopted Baumgarten's book as the text of his lectures. Kant's idea of identifying transcendental philosophy with ontology or general metaphysics, and of making his *Critique of Pure Reason* the preliminary to metaphysics, is a consequence of Baumgarten's theory. If we take into account the fact that Kant's criticism of metaphysics is directed against Baumgarten's rationalistic metaphysics, we shall avoid the fallacy of taking Kant's critique to be the absolute denial of metaphysics.

[1] *Ibid.*, para. 369.
[2] *Ibid.*, para. 305.
[3] *Ibid.*, para. 599.
[4] *Ibid.*, para. 600.

CHAPTER III

KANT AND METAPHYSICS

I. THE STAGES OF KANT'S PHILOSOPHY

There are two opposite interpretations of Kant's philosophy. The one takes it to be the foundation of natural science, and values it for its rejection of metaphysics; the other takes it to be a first step towards the establishment of a new metaphysics. The one is held by neo-Kantians, [1] who were influenced by 19th century positivism, the other by Paulsen, M. Wundt, Heimsoeth, Heidegger etc. [2] M. Wundt goes so far as to assert that Kant's contemporaries and followers generally held the second interpretation. [3] But although it is true that Kant's successors, e.g. Fichte and Schelling, tended towards metaphysics, there are no sufficient grounds for the assertion that they thought him to be a pioneer of new metaphysics. Hegel, for example, in the preface to the first edition of his *Science of Logic*, [4] published in 1812, said that German philosophy had been revolutionised during the previous 25 years. This was certainly a reference to the influence of the second edition of the *Critique of Pure Reason;* and Hegel went on to harshly reproach Kant's theory for making the German nation lose their interest in metaphysics. In his lectures on the history of philosophy, Hegel also accused Kant of shallowness and cowardliness in giving up thought for emotion. [5] Hegel's view was that the *Critique* gained its many supporters not by offering them anything positive but by e-mancipating them at a stroke from the old metaphysics. [6] He called Kant a repudiator of metaphysics like Jacobi, [7] and although we must allow for some rhetorical exaggeration, remembering that Hegel was

[1] H. Cohen, *Kants Theorie der reinen Erfahrung*, 1871; W. Windelband, *Geschichte der neueren Philosophie*, 1878; E. Cassirer, *Das Erkenntnisproblem in der Philosophie und Wissenschaft der neueren Zeit*, 1906; *Kants Leben und Lehre*, 1918; B. Bauch, *Immanuel Kant*, 1911, Leipzig, Berlin 1921; R. Kroner, *Von Kant bis Hegel*, 1921–4; K. Vorländer, *Immanuel Kant*, 1917, etc.

[2] F. Paulsen, *Immanuel Kant*, 1893; M. Wundt, *Kant als Metaphysiker*, 1924; Heimsoeth, *Studien zur Philosophie Immanuel Kants*, 1956; Heidegger, *Kant und das Problem der Metaphysik*, 1929; B. Martin, *Immanuel Kant, Ontologie und Wissenschaftstheorie*, 1951.

[3] Wundt, *op. cit.*, 3.

[4] Hegel, *Wiss. der Log.*, W. W. IV. 13.

[5] Hegel, *Vorlesungen ü.d. Gesch. d. Philosophie*, 2nd. ed., p. 486.

[6] *Ibid.*, 550.

[7] *Ibid.*, 551.

very proud of his completion of a new metaphysics, this is nonetheless a remarkable testimony to the way in which Kant was interpreted by his contemporaries. To take Kant as an opponent of metaphysics is not a recent misinterpretation by neo-Kantians, but perhaps the general view of Hegel's or even of Kant's contemporaries.

At any rate, as the disagreement in interpretation mentioned above reflects the opposition between empiricism and rationalism, the main currents of modern thought, and, as Kant himself was engaged in the synthesis of this opposition, it is perhaps inevitable that Kantian interpretations should diverge again. And we suspect moreover that the divergence suggests the incompleteness of Kant's solution with regard to the antagonism of empiricism and rationalism.

There is no doubt that Kant's main interest was metaphysics. This is quite evident from the frequent appearance of the word in his works, to say nothing of his official position as a professor of logic and metaphysics. Any unprejudiced reader of Kant's works must admit that the absolute denial of metaphysics was neither the intention nor the issue of Kant's philosophy. Kant's task, as a philosopher, was actually restricted to the criticism and reconstruction of metaphysics. This is natural enough, for in the tradition of pre-Kantian philosophy metaphysics was either synonymous with philosophy or at least formed its main part. The point, therefore, at which the rival interpretations part company is whether to find the essence of his philosophy in criticism (of knowledge) or in the end of criticism; in other words, whether criticism is the substitute for metaphysics or the preparation for some new metaphysics. The first interpretation, neglecting the new metaphysics, which Kant, in spite of his original intention, never completed, finds the whole significance of his work in criticism. The second interpretation, on the contrary, regards criticism as a preliminary to the new metaphysics, which Kant himself planned but left to be accomplished by posterity, and sees him as a pioneer of metaphysics.

As is well known, Kant started from the philosophy of the Leibniz-Wolff school. His thought is usually divided into pre-critical and post-critical periods. [1] The dividing point is the inaugural essay of 1770, *De Mundi Sensibilis atque Intelligibilis Forma et Principiis*. This division is

[1] The distinction is due to Kant himself. But, if we examine the development of his thought in more detail, there are several stages both in pre- and post-critical periods. The pre-critical period may be divided into at least two stages: the period of mathematical and natural science in the 1750's and the sceptical empiricist period in the 1760's The post-critical period may be divided also into two by the completion of the *Critique of Pure Reason* in 1781. Cf. Überweg-Moog, *G. d. Ph.*, III, 12th edn. p. 509 f. and Paulsen, *op. cit.*, p. 74 ff.

based upon his own acknowledgement that he was awoken from the dogmatic slumber of rational metaphysics by Hume's empirical theory. [1] At first glance it seems as if with this turning point he broke off decisively from metaphysics and tended towards a theory of empirical knowledge. This is, however, not the case. Kant's main interest in the first half of his pre-critical period was confined to natural science, while he had already begun to doubt metaphysics in the second half of this period. Kant, on the other hand, remained throughout his life a professor of metaphysics and repeated his lectures on metaphysics using Baumgarten's textbook. [2] These facts show us that Kant did not abandon Wolffian metaphysics completely, to say nothing of metaphysics in general. Wolff's theory aimed at giving experience conceptual form. It was developed by his school into radical logicalism. This school dominated German philosophy during Kant's boyhood, viz. from the 1720's to the 1730's but, owing to its sterile formalism it gradually decayed and gave way to Crusius' voluntaristic realism. [3] In addition to this, Newton's scientific theory, which was introduced into Germany at the beginning of the 1740's, diminished interest in metaphysics, which confined itself to the explanation of concepts, and accelerated the decay of Wolff's school. In this situation, Kant's mission was to save German traditional metaphysics from total decay and to make it come to terms with the natural science newly introduced from abroad.

The idea that intelligible being was the ground of the sensible world was already held by Kant in his pre-critical period. But the metaphysical foundation of the natural world only became a problem for him in 1756, when he began to lecture on metaphysics, using Baumgarten's text. In the two habilitation essays *Nova Dilucidatio*, 1755 and *Monadologia Physica*, 1756, Kant tried to reconcile Newton's physics with Wolff's metaphysics, taking Crusius into consideration as well. No doubt, Kant in this period adhered to Wolff's metaphysical theory. This was by no means an uncritical obedience, but a defence of traditional metaphysics against empiricism and realism, though the positive consequences of the latter are taken into account.

After that, Kant was influenced more profoundly by English and

---

[1] *Prol.* Works IV., 260. Hume's influence was mainly confined to the problem of causality. It was not the turning point, the great light of 1769. Cf. M. Wundt, *op. cit.*, pp. 137 f. and 159 ff.

[2] Baumgarten, A., *Metaphysica*, 1739.

[3] The work of Crusius which Kant first met with was only the *Abhandlungen über Gebrauch und Grenzen des Satzes vom bestimmenden Grunde*. Kant's two essays *Monadologia Physica*, 1756 and *Nova Dilucidatio*, 1755 were written to protect Wolff's theory against this. Cf. M. Wundt, *op. cit.*, p. 121 f.

French thought, and at the same time continued to study Crusius. Through these influences he came nearer than ever to realism, and inclined to the denial of the old metaphysics, attaching much importance to empirical science. *Dreams of a Spirit Seer*, 1766, [1] a criticism of Swedenborg's mysticism, is the representative work of this sceptical period. In this book, Kant took the view that the metaphysician was a man who dreams with his reason, like the spiritualist, and that metaphysical knowledge was of no practical use. This criticism is so radical that it seems to result in the total denial of metaphysics. And one may, like Paulsen, [2] regard this denial as a summit from which Kant's critical philosophy was a regress. But to remain sceptical was not in Kant's character. The denial of metaphysics was only a 'negative moment' towards higher affirmation.

After several years of meditation Kant thought that he had found a way of rescuing metaphysics. This is why his inaugural essay, *De Mundi* etc., 1770, is such a significant stage in his development. The turning point in his thought, which Kant called "the great light of 1769" [3] was, so Wundt conjectures, inspired by his study of Plato through Brucker's *History of Philosophy*. [4] In this essay, Kant, following Plato, divided the faculty of knowledge into Sense and Understanding, allotting phenomena to the former and things in themselves to the latter. Metaphysics was explained as a function of Understanding independent of experience, its object being the first principles of pure Understanding. Unlike Leibniz, Kant found a qualitative difference between Sense and Understanding. This is an important idea, which continues into the *Critique of Pure Reason*. But there were not yet the distinctions between Understanding and Reason, and between Categories and Ideas. The theory of knowledge and the foundations of metaphysics were only completed in his main work, which appeared ten years later.

During this period eclecticism and scepticism came more and more into vogue, and the naturalistic materialism of the French Encyclo-

---

[1] *Träume eines Geistersehers, erläutert durch Träume der Metaphysik*, 1765. This work was inspired by disappointment in Swedenborg's *Arcana Coelestia*, 8 Vols., 1749–1756, which Kant read with the highest hopes and expectations.
[2] Paulsen, *op. cit.*, p. 239 f.
[3] "Das Jahr 69 gab mir grosses Licht," *Refl.* 4; *Briefe* an J. H. Lambert d. 2ten Sept. 1770.
[4] J. Brucker, *Historia critica philosophiae*, 2nd. ed., 1766/67. Cf. *K.p.V.*, W.W. IV, p. 201. As to the "great light," there are other interpretations beside Wundt's, which we adopt. Paulsen and Adickes attributed it to Hume's influence, Vaihinger to Leibniz, and K. Fischer denied any outside influences. Cf. Wundt, *op. cit.*, p. 158 ff.; Paulsen, *Versuch einer Entwicklungsgeschichte der Kantischen Erkenntnistheorie*, pp. 126 ff; Adickes, *Kant Studien*, pp. 138 ff; Windelband, *Gesch. d. neueren Philosophie*, 6th edn., pp. 31 ff.; Vaihinger, *Komm*. I.

pedists was widely favoured. As is well known, Kant, in the preface
to the first edition of the *Critique of Pure Reason*, described this trend
in a highly metaphorical passage. For an unprejudiced reader, a glance
at this preface would be enough to show that Kant's true intention in
this work consisted not in the denial of metaphysics, but in its succour
and restoration. He wanted to reconstruct a metaphysical system by
making clear the reasons for which the old metaphysics has declined.
Metaphysics was a disposition [1] of human nature, and the task of
philosophers was to make a science out of this disposition. The *Critique
of Pure Reason* was explicitly characterised as "a necessary preparation
for the foundation of metaphysics as a science," [2] or "an enterprise to
reverse the traditional method of metaphysics." [3] Similarly, the theme
of the *Prolegomena* was the question "How is metaphysics as a science
possible?" [4]

The *Critique of Pure Reason* has two main parts: the Theory of Principles and the Theory of Method. The Theory of Principles is divided
into Aesthetic and Logic, of which the latter further subdivides into
Analytic and Dialectic. Now the Aesthetic and the Analytic (Logic)
are the foundation of, or the inquiry into, mathematics and natural
science, while metaphysics is the subject of the Dialectic (Logic). If the
Critique of Pure Reason is to be regarded as the theory of (empirical)
knowledge, the Aesthetic and the Analytic must be taken to be its
main parts, but if on the contrary it is to be taken as an inquiry into
metaphysical method, then the weight of the Dialectic must surpass the
other parts. The extensiveness of the latter seems to suggest its comparative importance. The Theory of Method is often assumed to be
superfluous, but this view is untenable because the Theory of Method
contains some important ideas which later develop into the *Critique
of Practical Reason* and the *Critique of Judgement*.

The Aesthetic and the Analytic aim at distinguishing the world of
appearance from the intelligible world, and at explaining our scientific
knowledge as consisting in the application of the concepts of the Understanding to sensible intuition. Experience is thus confined to the world
of appearance. But this does not mean that Kant denied the existence
of intelligible being. Rather, the assumption that intelligible being
underlay appearance was Kant's consistent view. In the Dialectic,

---

[1] *K.r.V.*, 1 rst. edn. W.W. IV, 4, 517; *Prol.*, W.W. IV, 279, 327. Anm. 353, 362; *K.r.V.*
2nd. edn. W.W. III, p. 21.

[2] *K.r.V.*, Vorr., 2. 2nd. edn. W.W. III, 21.

[3] *K.r.V.*, Vorr. XXIII, W.W., III, p. 15.

[4] *Prolegomena*, W.W. IV, pp. 365–371.

which deals with metaphysics, Kant distinguished the Idea or the Concept of Pure Reason from the Category [1] or the Concept of Pure Understanding, and laid down the right and wrong uses of Ideas. The right use was the ascending or regulative one, which starts from experience and regresses to principles, while the wrong use is the descending or constructive one, which starts from principles and predicts appearances. The dialectical inferences derived from the misuse of Ideas show us the limits of Pure Reason in its theoretical use, and the positive function of Ideas is entrusted to the Postulate of Practical Reason. In the Theory of Method, the traditional ideas of God, Freedom and Immortality are acknowledged as the chief objects of metaphysics; their significance however is confined to their role in the sphere of morality. The objective reality of the intelligible world is thus retained only as a moral belief. The *Critique of Pure Reason* was undertaken at first as a single Critique and was thought to be the groundwork for the metaphysics of both nature and morality. But Kant gradually became aware of its deficiency, and supplemented it with the second and the third Critiques. When these three Critiques were completed, the function of the first Critique was confined to the criticism of Theoretical Reason, and became the foundation of the Metaphysics of Nature, while the *Critique of Practical Reason* became the foundation of the Metaphysics of Morality. The *Critique of Judgement* played a somewhat different role. It had to act as liaison between the two other Critiques and was not the foundation of any special Metaphysics. [2]

According to Wundt, through the completion of the three Critiques, the *Critique of Pure Reason*, which was at first intended as a foundation, became itself the main edifice, and the incomplete plans for a superstructure of metaphysics proper came to appear mere supplements. The aim changed from giving *new foundations* to metaphysics to giving foundations to *new metaphysics*. [3] We must admit that through the completion of the three Critiques the balance of Kant's system changed, and the weight of the Critiques in his system increased. Hence it was natural for an interpretation to arise which restricted the significance of Kant's philosophy to criticism.

However, even if Kant was joking when he referred to the unfinished manuscripts, which had a provisional title *The Process from Metaphysical Principles of Natural Philosophy to Physics*, as his "life

[1] Cf. *Fortschr.* W.W. VIII, p. 304. Kant attributed categories to Aristotle, ideas to Plato. This is the traditional theory of Neo-Platonism.

[2] *K.U.*, W.W., V. p. 176.

[3] Wundt, *op. cit.*, 375 ff.

work," [1] there is a lot of other evidence that Kant thought of criticism as the mere laying of foundations on which metaphysics could and should be built. For instance, in the introduction to the second edition of the *Critique of Pure Reason* he characterises the Critique as a preliminary science to the system of Pure Reason. [2] And at the end of the *Critique of Judgement* he says that "The task of Criticism is over, let us proceed to doctrine." [3]

The upper storeys of Kant's architectonics consist in *The Metaphysical Principles of Natural Science* [4] based on Theoretical Reason, and *The Metaphysics of Morality*, [5] based on Practical Reason. The latter is divided into two parts: *The Metaphysical Principles (Anfangsgründe) of Legal Philosophy* and *The Metaphysical Principles of Moral Theory*. The plan belonging to the metaphysics of nature remained uncompleted, [6] and the *Foundation of Metaphysics of Morality* is more an early draft of the *Critique of Practical Reason* than an upper storey. [7]

Kant explains [8] that the plan of his philosophy consists in giving answers to the following problems: (1) What can I know? (Metaphysics); (2) What should I do? (Moral Philosophy); (3) What can I hope?; (4) What is man? *Religion within the Limits of Mere Reason* [9] belongs, so Kant tells us, to the third part of this plan. But it is not clear where the *Critique of Judgement* belongs. As we have said, Kant himself does not treat the *Critique of Judgement* as the foundation of any special metaphysics; but we find nevertheless some connection between the Philosophy of Religion and the third *Critique*, analogous, if not quite similar, to the relations between the *Metaphysics of Nature* and the first *Critique*, and between the *Metaphysics of Morality* and the second *Critique*. The *Critique of Judgement* may thus be assigned to the same part of the plan as the Philosophy of Religion. The work corresponding to the fourth question is, needless to say, *Anthropology from a Pragmatic Point of View*. [10] Only this is a somewhat popular lecture and cannot be thought of as the crown of Kant's philosophy. Besides these main works there are some small works useful to under-

[1] Hasse, *Letzte Äusserungen Kants von einem seiner Tischgenossen*, 21 ff.
[2] *K.r.V.*, Einl. pp. 24 ff. W.W. III, p. 42 f.
[3] *K.U.*, W.W., IX. p. 170. Cf. Wundt, *op cit.*, p. 281 f.
[4] *Metaphysische Anfangsgründe der Naturwissenschaften*, 1781.
[5] *Metaphysik der Sitten*, I., *Metaphysische Anfangsgründe der Rechtslehre*, II. *Metaphysische Anfangsgründe der Tugendlehre*, 1797.
[6] *Op. post.*, hrsg. v. Adickes, 1920, hrsg. v. Buchenau, 1936.
[7] *Grundlegung der Metaphysik der Sitten*, 1786. Cf. Wundt, *op. cit.*, p. 296 f.
[8] *Briefe* an C. Fr. Stäudlin, d. 4 Mai 1793.
[9] *Religion innerhalb der Grenzen der blossen Vernunft*, 1793.
[10] *Anthropologie in pragmatischer Hinsicht*, 1798.

standing Kant's view of metaphysics. These are *Prolegomena to All Possible Metaphysics as a Science* [1] and the prize essay set by the Berlin Academy of Sciences on the question: "What Progress has Metaphysics made in Germany since Leibniz and Wolff?" [2] The lectures on metaphysics [3] and the marginal notes [4] to Baumgarten's textbook on metaphysics also give us some useful suggestions.

2. CRITIQUE AND METAPHYSICS

According to Wolff, metaphysics was the science of being as a whole; it covered everything that could be conceived. It constituted the main part of philosophy, and only logic, practical philosophy, and knowledge of nature lay outside its province. Metaphysics was divided into Ontology, General Cosmology, and Theory of Spirit, the last being subdivided into Psychology and Natural Theology. The philosophers of Wolff's school fall into two groups according to their main interest, the one concerned with being in general, and the other with the principles of knowledge. The epistemological group, which was more powerful than the ontological, contained both Baumgarten and Knutzen, who was Kant's teacher. The weak point of Wolff's school, however, as Kant criticised it in Baumgarten, [5] was that they could not successfully define metaphysics by its generality alone. Generality does not suffice to distinguish metaphysical knowledge from experience. For even in empirical principles there is the difference between what is special and what is general. In consideration of this point, Hoffmann, [6] the teacher of Crusius, assigned special knowledge to metaphysics. According to him, philosophy is different from mathematics and art in that it is concerned with the nature of things. There are two kinds of philosophy, special philosophy and metaphysics. The one deals with the accidental construction of being, the other with what necessarily belongs to the world of possibility. The objects of metaphysics are Mind, Matter, Movement, Time, Cause, Effect, End, Means, Moral Law, etc. Crusius, [7] following Hoffmann, took over the old distinction between necessary

[1] *Prolegomena zu einer jeden künftigen Metaphysik, die als Wissenschaft wird auftreten können*, 1783.
[2] *Welches sind die wirklichen Fortschritte, die die Metaphysik seit Leibniz'ens und Wolff's Zeiten in Deutschland gemacht hat?* Hrsg. v. Rink, 1804.
[3] *Vorlesung über Metaphysik*, hrsg, v. Pölitz, 1821, Heinze, 1894.
[4] *Erläuterungen zur A. G. Baumgartens Metaphysica*, W.W., XVII.
[5] Kant, *K.r.V.*, 2nd. edn. W.W. III p. 545.
[6] A. F. Hoffman, *Vernunftslehre*, 1739, para. 2, p. 30.
[7] Crusius, *Entwurf der notwendigen Vernunft-Wahrheiten, wiefern sie den Zufälligen entgegen gesetzt werden*, para. 1–5.

and contingent truth, and maintained that metaphysics was concerned only with necessary truth. He excluded practical philosophy from metaphysics because in practical affairs he considered what was necessary to be inseparable from what was contingent. Mathematics, although its truths are necessary, was also excluded because of its special subject-matter. He followed Wolff's division of metaphysics but changed the order, putting ontology first, then theology, then cosmology, and lastly pneumatology. In all these branches metaphysics is mainly concerned with knowledge derived *a priori* from concepts. Crusius however could neither give a foundation to conceptual knowledge nor explain how necessary truth was possible. These were the problems left for Kant.

Kant's concept of metaphysics is due both to Wolff's school and to Crusius. The definition [1] of metaphysics as "The philosophy of the first grounds of our knowledge" (*Untersuchung über die Deutlichkeit der Grundsätze der natürlichen Theologie und der Moral. 2 Betr.*) is, without doubt, in accordance with Baumgarten, and also another definition: [2] "The philosophy which includes the highest principles governing the use of our understanding" (*De Mundi Sensibilis* etc.) These earlier concepts of metaphysics show a remarkable tendency towards the theory of knowledge later to be accomplished in the *Critique*. The most striking example of this tendency is to be found in the "Dreams," where metaphysics is characterised as "the science of the limits of human reason" rather than as "the knowledge of the attributes of things by reason." [3] It was not, however, Kant's real intention to drive metaphysics in this direction. More comprehensive definitions are to be found in the *Critique of Pure Reason*, such as "The totality of philosophical knowledge with systematic coherence acquired through Pure Reason," [4] or "The list of our whole property systematically organized and acquired from Pure Reason." [5] These definitions, like those of Crusius, are mainly concerned with the method of acquiring knowledge and do not mention the objects of knowledge. The definitions in the prize essay, "The system of all principles of the knowledge which is acquired from Pure Theoretical Reason through concepts," or more briefly, "The system of Pure Theoretical Philosophy," [6] are of the same kind.

---

[1] W.W. p. 283. Cf. Ref. N. 4853, N. 3952.
[2] *De mundi*, para. 8, W.W. II, p. 395.
[3] *Träume eines Geistersehers*, W.W. II, p. 368.
[4] *K.r.V.*, B. 869, W.W. III. 543 f.
[5] *K.r.V.*, XX, W.W. IV, 13.
[6] *Fortschritte* etc., Vorw. (Cass. ed.), W.W. VIII, p. 239, Beil. 303.

There are also definitions which mention the objects of knowledge. In the introduction to the *Critique of Pure Reason*, Kant explains that metaphysics is the science which has to solve the problems inevitable for Reason, i.e. God, Freedom, and Immortality. [1] In the Dialectic, he says that the proper objects of metaphysics are the three ideas: God, Freedom, and Immortality, the further problems being the means to reach these ideas and their reality. [2] Similarly in the *Prolegomena* metaphysics is said to be concerned both with the natural concepts usually applied to experience and with the concept of Pure Reason. [3] The principal objects of metaphysics are thus thought to lie outside possible experience. It is said that this part of metaphysics forms the essential end of the science, the others being only the means to attain this end. Likewise in the prize essay metaphysics is defined as the science which proceeds through Reason from the knowledge of sensible things to trans-sensible beings. [4]

From these definitions and explanations it is fairly evident that Kant considered the final end of metaphysics to be the knowledge of trans-sensible ideas. This fits the statement in the lectures on metaphysics, to the effect that metaphysics is the science outside and beyond the range of the natural sciences. [5] However, even if the final end of metaphysics is the knowledge of trans-sensible ideas, knowledge of sensible things is not thereby excluded from its domain. In fact, in its preliminary or applied parts metaphysics accepts natural concepts usually applied to experience, and these are its secondary objects. In the prize essay, after giving the definition already quoted, Kant goes on to say:

Ontology (as a part of metaphysics) is a system of all concepts of understanding and principles, insofar as these are given to sense, and are concerned with objects that may be experienced. It does not concern itself with trans-sensible objects, which, none the less, are the final end of metaphysics. Ontology, therefore, belongs to metaphysics merely as a preliminary science of metaphysics proper, as its porch or front garden. It is called transcendental philosophy, because it comprises the conditions of all knowledge *a priori* and its first elements. [6]

Whether ontology is a part of philosophy or its preliminary is not decided here; 'part' and 'preliminary' seem here to be treated as syno-

[1] *K.r.V.*, B. 7, W.W., III, p. 31.
[2] *Ibid.*, tr. Dial. I. B. 3, Abs. Anm. B. 395, W.W. III, p. 260.
[3] *Prol.* para. 40, W.W. IV, p. 327.
[4] *Fortschritte*, W.W. (Cass.) VIII, pp. 238, 302. Cf. *Prol.* para. 40, W.W. IV, p. 327.
[5] *Vorlesung über Met.*, ed. Heinze, p. 666.
[6] *Fortschritte*, W.W. (Cass.) VIII, p. 283.

nyms. Anyhow, though they are not the main objects of metaphysics, sensible things and their knowledge belong to metaphysics at least indirectly. We are reminded of the mediaeval distinction between the subject and the problem of metaphysics. [1] Of course it is very unlikely that Kant was conscious that this distinction originated from Avicenna. The analogy is nonetheless fairly plausible. The empirical entities dealt with by Kant's ontology correspond to the so-called subjects of metaphysics, and the three ideas, Kant's final ends, correspond to the problems. The former is the theme of Wolff's *metaphysica generalis*, the latter that of his *metaphysica specialis*. That Kant assumed the latter to be the proper objects of metaphysics implies that he thought of his Critique as a mere preliminary to *metaphysica specialis*.

"How is metaphysics possible as a science?": that was the main problem of Kant's philosophy. The problem presupposes that mankind is disposed towards metaphysics. In the "Dreams" this idea was at first expressed in the form of a personal confession made in a reserved tone: "The fate of being attracted with few rewards." [2] But in the *Critique of Pure Reason* Kant became more bold and declared metaphysics to be "the science necessary to human nature," [3] "necessary to the completion of the whole culture of human reason." [4] In the *Prolegomena* he is even more emphatic, calling it "the affectionate child of our reason," [5] and saying that "man can no more dispense with metaphysics than he can live without breathing." [6]

That mankind necessarily has a metaphysical disposition is not sufficient to prove that metaphysics is possible as a science. When this natural disposition is left uncultivated, it will lead to dialectic and fallacy. Therefore to establish a scientific metaphysics there must be a criticism of scientific knowledge. [7] "The Critique is to the school metaphysics of the past what chemistry is to alchemy, and what astronomy is to astrology. The old metaphysics is nothing but a sophistical pseudo-science." [8]

Metaphysics includes of course analytical judgements *a priori*, but, according to Kant, metaphysical knowledge in the proper sense must

---

[1] Cf. Chapter II, para. 2.
[2] *Träume*, W.W. II, p. 367.
[3] *K.r.V.*, Einl., B. 18, W.W. III, p. 39.
[4] *K.r.V.*, B. 878, W.W. III, p. 549.
[5] *Prol.* para. 57. W.W. IV, p. 353.
[6] *Ibid.*, *Auflösung d. all. Frage*, W.W. IV, 367.
[7] *Ibid.*, para. 60, W.W. IV, pp. 362 ff.
[8] *Ibid.*, W.W. IV, p. 366.

consist in synthetic judgements *a priori*. [1] In this respect, however, there is no difference between metaphysics and mathematics or natural science. The difference consists, Kant maintains, in the fact that, while mathematics can construct its object in intuition, metaphysics cannot, [2] and, while the natural sciences may apply the concepts of pure Understanding to sense-data, metaphysics, being devoid of such sense-data, [3] cannot form synthetic judgements *a priori*.

Neither pure mathematics nor pure natural science is concerned with transcendent being; they are concerned either with the conditions of possible experience or with what appears in some possible experience. [4] Whereas the proper objects of metaphysics are the absolute objects, viz., God, Freedom, and Immortality. This transcendent character of the objects, together with the lack of intuitive data, makes the demand of metaphysics for speculative knowledge impossible. An idea, which according to Kant means a concept of pure reason, distinct from any other empirical representation or even from any concept of pure understanding, must not be used constructively, but is only to be used regulatively. [5] In other words, it cannot give us any conception of an object. Its theoretical function is only to contribute towards the completion of our use of understanding in successive experiences, and its practical function is to act as a postulate and to give us rational belief or practical knowledge. [6] This is the final outcome of Kant's Critique.

The demand for criticism, as a way of raising metaphysics from the stage of mere disposition to the stage of science, arose from within metaphysics and was directed throughout by interest in metaphysics. [7] The Critique is therefore included in the system of critical metaphysics.[8] Now, as the first part of traditional metaphysics is ontology, Kant without hesitation identified his Critique with ontology. [9]

As for the various classifications of metaphysics, it is entirely to be

---

[1] *Prol.* para. 1 and 2, W.W. IV, p. 265 f.
[2] *K.r.V.*, Einl., p. 8 f, W.W. III, p. 31 f.
[3] *Prol.* para. 34 and 42, W.W. IV, 316, 329.
[4] *Ibid.*, para. 30, W.W. IV, p. 312 f.
[5] *K.r.V.*, tr. Dial. 2 B. H. 8. Abs. B. p. 536, W.W. III, pp. 348 ff; B. 672. W.W. p. 427; B. 699 ff. W.W. 443 ff; B. 730, W.W. 460.
[6] *K.r.V.*, tr. Dial. 2. B. 3. H. Abs., W.W. III, 420 ff; *Meth.* B. pp. 823 ff. W.W. III, 517; *K.p.V.*, 1. I. 2. B. 2 H. IV, W.W. V. pp. 122 ff.
[7] *Prol.* para. 57, W.W. IV, p. 353.
[8] *K.r.V.*, tr. Meth. 3. H. B. p. 869, W.W. III, 543 f.
[9] Ontology is transcendental philosophy, *Fortsch.* W.W. (Cass.) VIII, p. 328; and transcendental philosophy is the *Critique of Pure Reason, ibid.*, p. 251. Cf. *K.r.V.* B. p. 303, W.W. III, p. 207; B. p. 873, W.W. III, p. 546.

expected that the one in the lectures [1] on metaphysics is the most traditional. Metaphysics is here divided into *metaphysica pura* and *metaphysica applicata;* the former is subdivided into three parts: *ontologia, cosmologia,* and *theologia naturalis;* the latter into *somatalogia rationalis* and *psychologia rationalis.* The only difference from Wolff's classification is that *psychologia rationalis* is removed to *metaphysica applicata.*

A new attempt at classification appeared in the *Critique of Pure Reason.* [2] Corresponding to the speculative and practical uses of reason, metaphysics was divided here into Metaphysics of Nature and Metaphysics of Morals. The one involves all the principles of Pure Reason which concern the theoretical knowledge of anything from mere concepts, the other involves those principles which necessitate lines of conduct. Of the two, the metaphysics of speculative reason is what is regularly called metaphysics, i.e. in the narrower sense. The idea of practical metaphysics is peculiar to Kant. He explains this division with reference to the traditional classification: [3] "Metaphysics of Nature explains everything insofar as it exists, *a priori*, from concepts." "It consists in transcendental philosophy and physiology of pure reason." Transcendental philosophy is concerned with Understanding and Reason in the system of all concepts and principles, of objects in general without admitting any particular object, and this part of metaphysics is ontology. Physiology observes nature or the totality of objects given (to sense, or, if any, to another kind of intuition). It is therefore physiology, though rational. This rational physiology is either immanent or transcendent. The former is subdivided into rational physics and rational psychology, the latter into transcendental knowledge of the world and transcendental knowledge of God. Metaphysics therefore is divided into (1) Ontology; (2) Rational Physiology; (3) Rational Cosmology; and (4) Rational Theology. Compared with the classification in the lectures on metaphysics, the difference is that Rational Somatology, which was in the lectures counted as applied metaphysics, forms here the second part of metaphysics as a branch of Rational Physiology. Transcendental Philosophy is identified with Ontology, and forms the first part of metaphysics.

'Ontology,' 'Transcendental Philosophy,' and 'Critique' were used by Kant nearly synonymously, though with some slight difference in

---

[1] *Vorlesung ü. Met.* ed. Heinze, p. 667.
[2] *K.r.V.*, B. p. 869, W.W. III, p. 543 f.
[3] *Ibid.*, B. p. 873, W.W. III, p. 546 f.

their range. He invented the concept of Transcendental Philosophy as well as the distinction between 'transcendent' and 'transcendental.' [1] But the term *transcendentalia* may be traced back to Boethius. [2] Kant himself admitted [3] the historical existence of transcendental philosophy as a science of transcendent being, but thought it unworthy of the name. For, according to Kant, while a proper transcendental philosophy should *precede* metaphysics, what was traditionally called transcendental philosophy was rather a *part* of metaphysics. [4] This account, which we find in the *Prolegomena*, proves that Kant is claiming for transcendental philosophy both independence from and precedence over metaphysics. But it shows us also the pedigree of Kant's transcendental philosophy. On the one hand it is Criticism, on the other hand Ontology; on the one hand theory of knowledge, on the other metaphysics. Kant's Critique was not a criticism of metaphysics from the outside, like the criticism offered by present-day analytical philosophers and logical positivists. It was an offspring of metaphysics and aimed at its revival. Interpretations of Kant's philosophy will diverge in proportion to the importance attached to Kant's insistence on the independence of Criticism from metaphysics, and the identification of Criticism with Ontology. The origin of the divergence may be found in Wolff's classification of metaphysics, where Ontology, which, as a science of being in general, originally meant the same as metaphysics, was restricted to a mere preliminary part of metaphysics, the main part being constituted by *metaphysica specialis*. The divergence may be reduced to the mediaeval distinction between the subject and the object, and further to Aristotle's opposition between metaphysics as a science of being and metaphysics as theology. A similar correspondence is to be found in the two uses (*Vorteile*) [5] of metaphysics, of which Kant talks in his "Dreams" – namely the discovery of the concealed attributes of things through Reason, and the establishment of a limit to human Reason. The first is the doctrinal part of metaphysics, the second the preliminary part, i.e. Critique or transcendental philosophy.

The idea of identifying criticism or transcendental philosophy with ontology may be regarded as a development of Baumgarten's dis-

[1] *K.r.V.*, Einl. VII. B. p. 25, W.W. III, 43; *ibid.*, *tr. Log.* Einl. II, B. pp. 79 ff. W.W. III, p. 77 f.
[2] Boethius, *De Consol. philosph.* V., cf. Augustinus, *De vera relig. 72*, *De civitate Dei*, VIII, 6; St. Thomas, *Summa Th.*, I. 1.5., etc.
[3] *K.r.V.*, B. p. 113, W.W. III, p. 97.
[4] *Prolegomena*, para. 5, W.W. IV, p. 279.
[5] *Träume*, II. 2. W.W. II, p. 367.

tinction between metaphysics as the science of human knowledge, and ontology as the science of general predicates. Transcendental philosophy was defined in the prize essay [1] as the system of categories and principles governing sensible and empirical objects, a system which is the result of the immanent use of reason explained in the Aesthetic and the Analytic. Is this science a part of metaphysics proper, or is it a theory of knowledge lying outside metaphysics? The answer to this question will determine the character of Kant's philosophy. It is also connected with the problem of Hegel's interpretation of the relation between metaphysics and logic. Perhaps an inquiry into the origin of the Critique will give us the answer.

3. THE STAGES OF METAPHYSICS

It is true that ontology before Kant was merely a part of metaphysics without any taint of scepticism; it was an intrinsic part of metaphysics. But criticism of metaphysics did not abruptly appear from outside. [2] The progress of empirical knowledge was indeed a stimulus which drew attention to the poverty of metaphysics, but English empiricism and French positivism were of essentially alien blood to metaphysics. However, the metaphysical spirit of the German nation was dormant rather than dead, and with Kant's criticism it came to life again. But for the "natural disposition towards metaphysics," but for the "fate of unrewarded attraction to metaphysics," criticism as transcendental philosophy would not have come into existence. Transcendental philosophy, which had been the unreflective doctrine of transcendent being, became the criticism of metaphysical thinking, and Ontology became a preliminary to critical metaphysics. Seen from the standpoint of the old metaphysics, transcendental philosophy functioned only negatively, but, seen from that of the new metaphysics, it appeared as an indispensable condition of its existence. [3]

The Critique originates in metaphysics and becomes a part of the new metaphysics. [4] Towards the despotism of dogmatic metaphysics it is a judge from outside, but in the newly constituted state of metaphysics it takes its place as a good citizen. The process of this transition may be understood through observation of the stages of metaphysics. In the preface to the first edition of the *Critique of Pure Reason*, Kant

---

[1] *Fortschritte*, W.W. (Cass.) VIII. p. 238.
[2] *Prol.* para. 57, W.W. IV, p. 351.
[3] *K.r.V.*, Vorr. B. XXIV ff, W.W. III, p. 16 f.
[4] *K.r.V.* tr. *Meth.* 3 H.B. p. 869, W.W. III, p. 543 f.

describes the development of metaphysics with an allegorical touch. He says that the despotism of the dogmatists fell into anarchy due to a rebellion, the unity of te citizens was destroyed by the sceptics, a kind of nomad, and the indifferentism resulting from this confusion made it necessary to establish a court,[1] viz., the Critique of Pure Reason. The same idea is expounded in the theory of method, and also appears in a more refined form in the prize essay[2]

In the prize essay, the development of metaphysics was also divided into three stages: dogmatism scepticism, and criticism. English scepticism as well as Kant's own criticism was not excluded from the range of metaphysics. Both were regarded as forming the reflective stage of Pure Reason for the sake of metaphysics, themselves being a stage of the development of metaphysics. Dogmatism included all the systems of metaphysics, from Plato and Aristotle to Leibniz and Wolff, its essence being regarded as unreflective reliance on Reason. Scepticism resulted from the failures of all these metaphysical systems, but, though it duly pointed out the paradox of Reason, its contentions against empirical knowledge were not taken seriously, and it could only ask dogmatism to prove the principles of experience. Criticism was placed between dogmatism and scepticism. Its role was to determine the range, content, and limit of both doctrines for the sensible and trans-sensible worlds.

The three stages were explained somewhat differently in the main discourse.[3] These are: (1) theoretical-dogmatic advance; (2) sceptical halt; and (3) practical-dogmatic completion. That Dogmatism is to be characterised as a theoretical-dogmatic advance and Scepticism as a halt, we can agree to without argument. The difficulty is as to whether what was previously called critical is the same as what is now called practical-dogmatic completion. Insofar as criticism is assumed to form the stage after scepticism, then it is not a mere negative halt, but a positive establishment of something. Consequently there is no real inconsistency in its being called a completion. To call it practical suggests, as we shall explain later, the positive outcome of Kant's Critique. But what appears strangest is the fact that the stage which was previously called critical is now characterized[4] as dogmatic, for a dogmatic criticism would be a sheer *contradictio in adjecto*. Does this then suggest an oscillation in Kant's thought? – By no means. Another

[1] *K.r.V.*, Vorr. A. IX. f. W.W. IV, p. 8.
[2] *K.r.V.*, B. pp. 789 ff. W.W. III, pp. 497 ff.
[3] *Fortsch.* W.W. (Cass.) VIII, p. 240 f.
[4] *Ibid.*, pp. 264 ff.

hypothesis was made by M. Wundt, [1] to the effect that Kant assumed himself to be a dogmatist. – To say so much is surely an exaggeration. The key to the question is the meaning of the word 'dogmatic.' For Kant, being dogmatic did not necessarily imply being a dogmatic in the bad sense. Rather, in accordance with its original meaning, 'dogmatic' is only used to mean *positive* knowledge as against *negative* criticism; and this use must be strictly distinguished from the ordinary use of 'dogmatic' to mean 'uncritical.' According to Kant, 'dogmatic' meant "the way to prove something from certain principles *a priori*," whereas dogmatism is "the dogmatic way of Pure Reason to recognize something without being preceded by any criticism of its ability." [2] Hence we see that the third stage of metaphysics, i.e. the practical-dogmatic stage, does not involve a return to dogmatism in the bad sense, but is just a practical use of Reason in positive activity, starting from certain principles *a priori*. There is therefore no contradiction to be feared between the two different characterizations of the third stage. What must be borne in mind, however, is that criticism was not only a limitation of theoretical Reason, but also afforded practical Reason a positive activity.

Kant compared these three stages to the three parts of metaphysics, viz., ontology, cosmology, and theology. [3] But this seems, I confess, to be a somewhat forced argument. If this correspondence is admitted, the three stages of metaphysics must be taken as a logical construction instead of a temporal development – which would upset the original idea. [4] Though we agree with Wundt in the assumption that Kant's Critique acquired a positive significance through the completion of the other two Critiques, we cannot follow Wundt in arguing, on the basis of the alleged correspondence, that Kant changed his views on metaphysics. The attempt to correlate the parts of metaphysics with the stages of its development must be treated as a bad example of Kant's architectonic way of thinking. The alleged correspondence lacks the character of necessity, so that no good result can be expected from any criticism based upon it. How, for example, does theoretical-dogmatic advance correspond to ontology? This does not square with the idea of identifying ontology with transcendental philosophy or criticism. How does sceptical halt correspond especially to cosmology? The antinomy, to be sure, is a remarkable phenomenon of transcen-

---

[1] Wundt, *op. cit.*, p. 387.
[2] *K.r.V.*, Vorr. B. XXXV, W.W. III. 21. Cf. Buchenau, *Grundprobleme der K.r.V.*, p. 13 f.
[3] *Fortsch.*, W.W. (Cass.) VIII, p. 262 ff.
[4] Wundt, *op. cit.*, p. 389.

dental dialectic, but there are also other forms of dialectic than the antinomy, viz. the paralogism in psychology and the ideal in theology. How, further, does dogmatic completion correspond particularly to theology? Is there no practical dogmatic performance outside the range of theology? In short, taking into account the fact that the work was never published, the alleged correspondence is best regarded as a mere *Gedankenexperiment*.

Anyhow, the theme of the first stage, theoretical-dogmatic advance, is the analysis of the concepts of Pure Understanding and the conditions of their application to experience. It corresponds to the analytic of Pure Reason. In this stage, Kant acknowledges the merit of Leibniz and Wolff. What Kant takes to be their defect is that they ignored pure intuition and explained the possession of knowledge only from the possession of the concepts of Understanding. This obliged them, so argues Kant, to accept many unreasonable principles such as the principle of the identity of indiscernibles, the principle of sufficient reason, the principle of pre-established harmony and the theory of monadology. Let us, for the moment, leave on one side the question whether or not this stage should be called ontology. There is certainly great merit in Kant's criticism of the dogmatic rationalism which constructs knowledge from mere concepts of the Understanding without sense data, assuming intuition to be a lower stage of understanding.

The second stage, sceptical halt, corresponds to cosmology. This section deals with the same topics as does the Dialectic in the *Critique of Pure Reason*, especially the antinomy. This is assumed to be the destiny of Pure Theoretical Reason when it is concerned with absolute being. Two kinds of antinomy are distinguished: the mathematical and the dynamic. The first concerns the opposition between the infinity and the finitude of the world in respect of time and space, and the opposition between the affirmation and negation of simple parts constituting compound substances. The other concerns the questions whether to admit causality through freedom or to deny it, confining causality to natural law, and the question whether to admit necessary being or not. The mathematical antitheses may be both false, while the dynamic antitheses may be both true, i.e. as *phenomena* they are false, but as *noumena* they are true. The cognition of *noumena*, however, is denied to theoretical reason; it is in some way revealed only to practical reason. It deserves our special attention that a transsensible knowledge about the final end of metaphysics is admitted though with some restriction.

Now to explain the sceptical halt thus by means of antinomy is not unreasonable, because the ruin of theoretical reason appears especially in the antinomy of cosmological ideas, though speaking strictly the transcendental dialectic is not just a discussion of cosmology, but also comprises the psychological and theological ideas.

The third stage of metaphysics is the standpoint of the new metaphysics acknowledged by Kant's critique. The prize problem of the Academy was concerned with the possibility of theoretical metaphysics viz., "A system of all principles of knowledge by pure theoretical Reason through concepts," or in short "a system of pure theoretical philosophy." To this question Kant gave a negative answer, but he affirmed the possibility of practical dogmatic advance concerning trans-sensible being. This is the metaphysics of morality as opposed to metaphysics of nature, the latter being rather theoretical science.

The concepts which are the final end of pure practical Reason are formed by Reason itself. They are God, Freedom, and Immorality. Kant considered it the final end of metaphysics to bring these trans-sensible ideas to practical dogmatic knowledge. His transcendental philosophy started from the sceptical halt and tended towards practical dogmatic advance. The Dialectic in the *Critique of Pure Reason* has a negative result, but the *Critique of Practical Reason* and the *Critique of Judgement* opened the way to a positive knowledge of metaphysics of morality.

A system of critical metaphysics now came into existence through the replacement of ontology by critique or transcendental philosophy, or rather making the latter into a new ontology. The Critique grew from doubts about the old metaphysics, but instead of denying metaphysics absolutely it became a preliminary to metaphysics as a science. The Critique restricted theoretical Reason and passed its objects to practical Reason, attributing the failure of the old metaphysics to the misuse of theoretical Reason.

4. THE SYSTEM OF CRITICAL METAPHYSICS

Let us take up again our consideration of the various classifications of metaphysics. The classification in the *Critique of Pure Reason* [1] is almost the same as that in the lectures on metaphysics. There were two kinds of metaphysics, the metaphysics of speculative Reason and the metaphysics of practical Reason. The one is also called metaphysics

---

[1] *K.r.V.*, B. pp. 869 ff. W.W. III, pp. 543 ff.

of nature, the other metaphysics of morality. The former is meta-physics in a narrower sense. It is subdivided into transcendental philosophy or ontology and physiology, of which the latter comprises immanent physiology and transcendental physiology. Immanent physiology is either rational physics or rational psychology; transcendent physiology is either rational cosmology or rational theology. We may represent it diagrammatically:

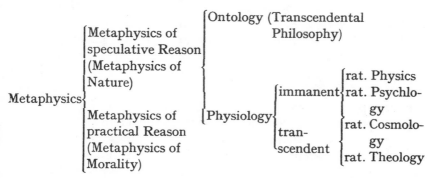

The main points to be investigated are as follows: (1) Is it correct to call metaphysics of speculative Reason metaphysics of nature, and to call metaphysics of practical Reason metaphysics of morality? (2) Does ontology or transcendental philosophy really constitute a part of the metaphysics of nature? In other words: Is this ontology the same as that ontology which precedes both the metaphysics of nature and the metaphysics of morality? (3) Is it consistent on the one hand to limit the speculative use of Reason to empirical knowledge and on the other hand to admit the metaphysics of speculative Reason? Further, how is it possible for rational psychology, rational cosmology and rational theology, which formed the *metaphysica specialis* in the traditional system, to fit into the system of new metaphysics?

The identification of speculative metaphysics and the metaphysics of nature on the one hand, practical metaphysics and metaphysics of morality on the other, may be found also in the prize essay. [1] In this essay, metaphysics as theoretical science is called metaphysics of nature and metaphysics as practical science is called metaphysics of morality. It is an ancient theory to give each object its special method and to deny e.g. practical knowledge of nature or speculative knowledge of morality. But even if this be admitted, since natural metaphysics cannot attain trans-empirical objects, there cannot be any

[1] *Fortsch.* W.W. (Cass.) VIII, p. 276.

possibility of rational cosmology or rational theology. And further, when we consider Kant's conclusion to the *Critique*, namely that the ideas of freedom, immortality, and God are the objects of mere practical belief or at most of practical knowledge, we clearly must regard the corresponding branches of metaphysics – rational psychology, rational cosmology, rational theology, etc. – as belonging to the metaphysics of morality.

As to the position of ontology, Kant says in the *Metaphysical Principles of Natural Science:* [1] "Metaphysics involves of necessity mainly principles which are not empirical . . . it also sometimes deals with the law which makes the concept of nature in general possible, without having any reference to a particular object of experience, and consequently without determining the qualities of individual things in the sensible world; in this case, it is the transcendental part of metaphysics of nature." Kant here does not mean, however, to make transcendental philosophy in general subordinate to metaphysics of nature, but rather means to admit a part of transcendental philosophy as the foundation of the metaphysics of nature. We might suppose that there is another part of transcendental philosophy which serves as the foundation of the metaphysics of morality. There is indeed a statement in the *Critique of Pure Reason* [2] to the effect that the highest principles and fundamental concepts of morality, though they are *a priori*, do not belong to transcendental philosophy, while transcendental philosophy is a philosophy of speculative reason. And this seems to run counter to our supposition. However, what this statement really means is that transcendental philosophy belongs to the function of speculative reason, not that metaphysics of morality needs no transcendental philosophy. In the introduction to the *Metaphysics of Morality*,[3] Kant maintained explicitly that the Metaphysics of Morality presupposed the Critique of Practical Reason just as Metaphysics presupposed the Critique of Pure Theoretical Reason. It may be noticed that the Critique of Pure Reason is here determined as theoretical, while the branch that is to be based upon this critique is merely called metaphysics without any special determination. Strictly speaking, however, it should be determined as natural metaphysics or metaphysics of nature. Otherwise the system would be asymmetrical and the two critiques would bear different relations to their dogmatic

[1] *Met. Anf. der Nat.*, Vorr., W.W. IV, p. 469.
[2] *K.r.V.*, B. p. 29, W.W. III, p. 45.
[3] *Gr. d. M.S.*, W.W. IV, p. 391.

superstructures. At first, the Critique of Pure Reason was regarded as a preliminary to metaphysics in general. But, due to the completion of the Critique of Practical Reason, it came to be regarded as the preliminary to metaphysics of nature only, while the Critique of (Pure) Practical Reason became the preliminary to metaphysics of morality. In short, in Kant's complete system, transcendental philosophy or ontology was divided into two parts; one was preliminary to the metaphysics of nature and the other to the metaphysics of morality. The first is the Critique of Pure (Theoretical) Reason, the second is the Critique of (Pure) Practical Reason. These two critiques, together with the Critique of Judgement, form the complete transcendental philosophy, the preliminary to metaphysics in general.

As for the third question, we would first call attention to the fact that not every part in the classification mentioned above was accepted by Kant as valid. These parts are what were called *Feld* in the *Critique of Judgement*, [1] not *Boden*, nor *Gebiet*. Rational Cosmology or Rational Theology is not a possible theoretical science. Even in immanent physics, rational psychology is impossible. [2] Rational Physics is the only possible dogmatic part of natural metaphysics. [3] The actual content of the metaphysical foundations of natural science according to Kant was only somatology. Psychology was considered impossible as an empirical science, since mathematics could not be applied to it. Psychology was no more than historical and descriptive knowledge, so less than a science in the strict sense. Transcendental psychology, on the other hand, which claimed to be knowledge underived from experience, necessarily fell into dialectic and fallacy through a wrong use of ideas and could not consequently form a real part of natural metaphysics. In his posthumous work, Kant intended to establish a system of knowledge of nature, which embraced all the special sciences. It was concerned with "the passage from the Metaphysical Principles of Natural Science to Physics" and was to include chemistry, electro-

---

[1] *K.U.*, Vorr., Einl. II, W.W. V, p. 174. Concepts, as far as they are referred to objects apart from the question of whether knowledge of them is possible or not, have their field, which is determined simply by the relation in which their object stands to our faculty of cognition in general. – The part of this field in which knowledge is possible for us, is a territory (*territorium*) for these concepts and the requisite cognitive faculty. The part of the territory over which they exercise legislative authority is the realm (*ditio*) of these concepts, and their appropriate cognitive faculty. Empirical concepts have, therefore, their territory, doubtless, in nature as the complex of all sensible objects, but they have no realm only a dwelling place (*domicilium*), for, although they are formed according to law, they are not themselves legislative, but the rules founded on them are empirical, and consequently contingent. (Meredith's tr.)

[2] *Met. Anf. d. Nat.*, Vorr. W.W. IV, p. 470 f.

[3] *Ibid.*, p. 469 f.

magnetic theory, biology etc., and all the latest discoveries of the natural sciences. But this work was left uncompleted.

The metaphysics of practical reason, or the metaphysics of morality, consists firstly in a critical part - the 'Critique of Practical Reason,' and its previous form, the 'Foundation of the Metaphysics of Morality' – and secondly in a dogmatic part – the 'Metaphysics of Morality,' a work in two parts, namely the 'Metaphysical Principles of Politics' and the 'Metaphysical Principles of the Theory of Virtue.' The function of mediating between theoretical Reason and practical Reason is given in the critical part to the *Critique of Judgement* and in the dogmatic part to *Religion within the Limits of Mere Reason*.

Metaphysics of Nature was divided into a transcendental part and a special part; the former dealt with the laws that made the concept of nature in general possible, the latter with the qualities of particular things, to which empirical concepts are applied. The transcendental part must be the Aesthetic and the Analytic in the *Critique of Pure Reason*, while the special part, instead of being called special metaphysics of nature, is called special metaphysical science of nature, to which would belong physics and psychology. Of these two possible branches of special metaphysics of nature, however, psychology is, as we have said, excluded in practice because it cannot be treated mathematically. Hence it is evident that the so-called metaphysics of nature consists in the application of metaphysical principles to natural science, and, since these metaphysical principles are given by the transcendental part of natural metaphysics, i.e. by the *Critique of Pure Reason*, this application is not a transcendent but an immanent use of pure theoretical reason, an application of the concepts and fundamental rules of the Understanding to nature as the empirical object in general.

The metaphysics of nature is, without doubt, the metaphysics of theoretical reason. But it must not be confused with the dogmatic metaphysics which consisted in undisciplined judgements resulting from an incorrect use of theoretical Reason and was rejected in the *Critique of Pure Reason*. The metaphysics of nature is rather a science derived from metaphysics, not a system of speculative knowledge about transcendent ideas, such as metaphysicians of the past indulged in. In the *Metaphysical Principles of Natural Science*, Kant says:

The end for which metaphysicians have taken and will also take pains is not for the sake of extending therewith the knowledge of nature, ...but rather for the sake of attaining the knowledge of what is quite beyond the limit of any experience, viz. the knowledge of God, freedom, and immortality. To attain this end, it is more expedient to promote the part which, although being an off-shoot from the root of metaphysics, is merely an obstacle for normal progress of metaphysics, i.e. general somatology, separately from the system of general metaphysics, without however losing its connection with the whole. [1]

The metaphysics of somatic nature, though an independent branch, certainly contributes to general metaphysics, which is in fact a transcendental philosophy, giving it examples, realizing its concepts and theorems and giving content to the mere form of thought.

The general part of natural metaphysics is transcendental philosophy; its special part is, so to speak, an applied metaphysics or metaphysical science of nature, which applies the concepts and fundamental rules of the Understanding to the objects of experience in general. The latter only makes a minor contribution to the proper end of metaphysics. But insofar as this metaphysical science of nature, which consists in the immanent use of theoretical reason, is called natural metaphysics, and forms the metaphysics of nature together with the Critique of Pure Reason, it implies a new interpretation of metaphysics on the part of Kant. [2] The first part of this new metaphysics covers the Critique of Pure Reason together with the basic theory of natural science – immanent metaphysics, which consists in the constructive use of concepts and fundamental rules acknowledged by the Critique. The second part of critical metaphysics contains the Critique of Practical Reason as its transcendental part, and the Metaphysics of Morality as its dogmatic part. This dogmatic part of practical metaphysics, however, has a content analogous to that of the *Metaphysical Principles of Natural Science* and does not contain a systematic knowledge *a priori* of God, freedom, and immortality. The answers to these traditional problems were given rather in the *Critique of Practical Reason*. Here is the peculiarity of the *Critique of Practical Reason* as compared to the *Critique of Pure Reason*. Being a critique of reason, it is surely a transcendental part of the metaphysics of morality. But unlike the *Critique of Pure Reason*, which has the purely negative function of showing the limits of theoretical reason, the *Critique of Practical Reason* claims that Reason has a positive function in its practical use. In this respect, it is at the same time both transcendental philosophy and dogmatic theory.

Thus, the proper problems of metaphysics were developed in the *Critique of Practical Reason* and also in the *Critique of Judgement*,

[1] *Ibid.*, p. 477 f.
[2] Cf. Paulsen, I. *Kant*, pp. 275 ff.

which combined and augmented the other two Critiques. Kant's
critical metaphysics was constituted by the first *Critique* as *metaphysica
generalis*, the second and the third *Critiques* as *metaphysica specialis*.
The metaphysics of nature and the metaphysics of morality, which
were at first planned to be *metaphysica specialis*, and were partly completed as such, finished up as an applied metaphysics of minor importance.

5. THE SUPREMACY OF PRACTICAL REASON AND THE POVERTY OF SPECULATIVE PHILOSOPHY

Since the 19th century, academic philosophy has divided itself into
three main parts: theory of knowledge, metaphysics or ontology, and
practical philosophy; all these three parts were, according to Kant,
comprised in metaphysics. "Theory of knowledge" was a new term in
the 19th century, [1] but Kant's *Critique of Pure Reason* was actually
the origin of this theory. Kant himself called it metaphysics of metaphysics, transcendental philosophy, or critique, and also identified it
with ontology. Whereas the academic philosophy of the 19th century
identified both metaphysics with ontology, and the critique with
the theory of knowledge, Kant himself never assumed his theory
of knowledge to be an end in itself, nor did he assume the foundation
of natural science to be the final end of his critique. The Metaphysics
of Nature was to be sure, the foundation of natural science, but
it was only a subordinate part of metaphysics. The deduction of
the categories in the *Critique of Pure Reason* was not necessary for
pure mathematics or pure natural science, but 'for another science,
viz., metaphysics.' [2] This metaphysics is 'the science which deals both
with natural concepts that are always applied to experience, and with
the concepts of Reason, which are never given in any possible experience.' [3] The results of pure natural science and pure mathematics
operate as a steady springboard for rational knowledge to make a new
jump. The aim of the *Critique* was to find the method and limits of
rational knowledge of trans-sensible objects. [4] This cannot be overlooked by anyone, since it is so often repeated by Kant himself. The
reason why interpreters have nevertheless inclined to treat Kant's

---

[1] I. H. Fichte, *Grundsätze f.d. Ph. d. Zukunft*, 1847; Zeller, *Über Bedeutung u. Aufgabe der Erkenntnistheorie*, 1862. Cf. Ueberweg-Oesterreich *G.d.G.d.Ph.* III, pp. 418 and 423.

[2] *Prol.* para. 40, W.W. IV, p. 327, para. 44 and 331.

[3] *Ibid.*, p. 327.

[4] *K.U.*, B. 7. W.W. III, p. 31. A. XII, W.W. IV. 7. B. XVI, W.W. III, p. 11 f.

philosophy as the theory of knowledge is that the *Critique* denied knowledge of transcendent being to theoretical reason and allowed it only to Practical Reason.

Essentially, metaphysics has been a theoretical science, systematic knowledge of speculative Reason. This is not a particular opinion of Wolff's school, but a traditional theory since Aristotle. If this traditional metaphysics is taken to be impossible, this practically amounts to the death of metaphysics in general even though some possibility is left to practical reason. Just like the concept of 'metaphysics of experience,' the concept of practical metaphysics is a *contradictio in adjecto*. To justify this strange concept, it is necessary to change the meaning of 'metaphysics.' Those who regarded Kant's Critique as the negation of metaphysics may have judged his philosophy by its outcome rather than by the intention of its author.

It is indeed a queer thought to take metaphysics to be impossible as theoretical knowledge but only possible as practical. For even though knowledge was in its origin a tool of practice, no one can deny that its ideal form is theoretical. It is commonly admitted that knowledge about matters of our immediate interest is practical, while knowledge of ideal objects of highly abstract form is theoretical. It is for this reason that Aristotle assumed pure form without matter, viz., God or Spirit, to be the object of theoretical knowledge. It was generally admitted that, since the objects of metaphysics are trans-sensible beings, the knowledge of them, if possible, must be theoretical. Kant's denial of this traditional idea was indeed a revolution, more striking even than his so-called Copernican revolution. It was therefore more difficult for the former to secure general approval than it was for the latter. In truth, there was no inconsistency between Kant's Copernican revolution and his Christian view of the world, for Kant confirmed the supremacy of mind over nature. It was quite in conformity with his lifelong view of the world since his adolescence – a view better called Ptolemaic than Copernican, as many critics have suggested. For in the Copernican view of the world the earth is a planet in the solar system, whereas in Kant's transcendental philosophy our mind is not a part of nature, but rather the ruler of nature. This is akin rather to Ptolemy's view of the world, in which all stars go around the earth. The only similarity between Kant's transcendental theory and Copernican astronomy is that both revolutionized previous thought. But the ways in which they did this were vastly different. Kant's theory of knowledge, which required nature to obey mind, could easily have been approved of even by Berkeley. [1] Copernican astronomy was a radical attack on the geocentric view of the middle ages, but Kant's transcendental philosophy might well be called a conservative reaction in the line of German mysticism and idealism, opposed to the new materialism, mechanism, and the Philosophy of the Enlightenment of England and France in the 17th and the 18th centuries.

The chief point of Kant's philosophy was the recognition of the supremacy of mind. As against Copernicus' bold idea that made our earth a small star in a huge system of matter, Kant's transcendental idealism aimed at the restoration of the reign of ideas which necessarily govern the whole material universe, the defence of the spiritual authority in its crisis of downfall.

For all that, Kant, who had been influenced by Newton's physical theory and the Philosophy of the Enlightenment, and had started his intellectual life as an excellent natural scientist, could by no means neglect the universal validity of natural laws. Hence, on the one hand he acknowledged nature in general to be a system in accordance with law, and on the other hand he believed in an intelligible order quite independent of the natural world – a modern specimen of the old double-world theory. He assured, so to speak, the peace of the spiritual kingdom by removing it from earth to heaven, and gave the key of that heaven to the moral imperative. For Kant, metaphysics was 'the fortress of religion ... it restricted reason and prevented the decay which unlawful speculation might bring about in the region of morality and religion.' [2]

By thus separating the intelligible from the sensible world, and restricting the knowledge acquired by the Understanding to the latter, it appeared as if he had secured a lasting peace between the two worlds. Natural science could develop in its own way free from spiritual interference. But this peace imposed severe restrictions on speculative reason. Kant's resignation from the attempts to construct theoretical metaphysics implied the complete defeat of speculative reason. When Kant emphasized that the object of experience must, for a human being, be given at first to sensible intuition, he affirmed in fact that we can only theoretically recognize material nature.

Kant did not consider this a complete denial of transsensible being,

[1] I would not ignore the fact that Kant distinguished his critical idealism from Berkeley's dogmatic idealism and Descartes' sceptical idealism. Cf. *Prol.* Anh., W.W. IV, p. 374.

[2] *K.r.V.*, B. p. 877, W.W. III, p. 548 f. cf. *ibid.*, B. XXX, W.W. III, p. 19. Ref. N. 4284, N. 4865.

for the latter was rescued through being removed from the theoretical to the practical sphere. Following the Christian Scholastic tradition, Kant found these trans-sensible natures in the ideas of God, freedom, and immortality. Seen from the standpoint of theoretical reason, these concepts were called ideas, from that of practical reason, postulates.[1] According to the Neo-Kantian interpretation, these are not existences, but only ideals, not *Sein* but *Sollen.* [2] God, freedom, and immortality, are not things which either exist or do not exist. They are only things which insofar as they are required are affirmed. Theoretical reason can neither prove nor disprove the existence of these ideas. The postulate of practical reason was protected through making theoretical reason abstain from such presumptuous judgements.

Now these beings are objects of faith [3] rather than of knowledge. Kant at first used the concept of knowledge strictly and confined it to the empirical use of theoretical reason, but with the *Critique of Practical Reason* he gradually enlarged its scope to cover the area of practice and called what he had at first called moral faith rational faith, and then finally practical knowledge. [4] In this last case, freedom as the fact of pure practical reason played the analogous part to that played by sensible intuition in theoretical knowledge. [5]

Kant believed he had succeeded in avoiding materialism and atheism by separating the material world from the spiritual world, nature from morality, restricting theoretical reason to empirical use, and allowing the supremacy of practical reason over theoretical reason. [6] By the 'supremacy of practical reason' he meant the supremacy of the interest of practical reason over the interest of theoretical reason. This is because every interest is in the end practical, and the interest of speculative reason depends upon and is accomplished by the practical use of reason. [7] The postulate of practical reason is a theoretical proposition inseparable from the practical law. It cannot be proved, as it is not a theoretical dogma but a presupposition necessary only from a practical point of view. It cannot enlarge our theoretical knowledge, but serves to give objective reality to the ideas of speculative reason

[1] *K.r.V.*, B. 661 ff. W.W. III, pp. 421 ff; *K.p.V.*, p. 220, W.W. V, pp. 122, 132 ff.
[2] Cf. *K.r.V.*, B. p. 661, W.W. III, p. 421.
[3] *K.U.*, para. 91. W.W. V, 469 f. *K.r.V.*, B. p. 856, W.W. III, p. 546.
[4] Wundt, *op. cit.* pp. 313 ff., cf. *G.M.S.*, W.W. IV, p. 462. "Was heisst: sich im Denken orientieren?" (1786) W.W., VIII, pp. 140 ff.
[5] Wundt, *op. cit.*, pp. 322 ff.
[6] *K.r.V.*, B. p. 421, W.W. III, p. 274 f. B. p. 668, W.W. p. 425 f. *Prol.*, Para. 60, W.W. IV, p. 363.
[7] *K.p.V.*, I. 2. 2. III, W.W. V, p. 120 f.

and to justify them as concepts. The postulates of God, freedom, and immortality are the practical imperatives *a priori*, their possibility can be neither explained nor proved. They are only required from a practical point of view as conditions which enable us to perform our duty, for what is morally imperative is necessarily a duty. [1]

The idea of the supremacy of practical reason may be regarded as a forerunner of pragmatism. It may lend some support to Vaihinger's notorious interpretation. But seen from a metaphysical point of view, it is indeed a vulgar conception. [2] If the supremacy of practical reason is to be maintained because every interest is essentially practical, then philosophy unavoidably becomes in the end a servant of theology and a tool of politics. No, philosophical interest requires on the contrary that reason should be independent of all practical interests. In the name of theoretical reason we are justified in asking not only whether Kant's three ideas are necessary for morality, but also whether morality itself is necessary. Just as Kant himself remarked in criticizing the so-called ontological proof of the existence of God, [3] that even if the concept of a God which does not exist may be contradictory to itself, we would not be involved in any contradiction, if we threw away the subject together with the contradictory predicate; so, in the same way, even if God, freedom, and immortality are necessary for a certain morality or even for morality in general, these ideas may be done away with by throwing away that morality or morality in general. Theoretical reason is ready to face even such complete nihilism. In fact both present-day existentialists and the atheists of the Enlightenment are daring enough to put forward arrogant views of this kind. I wonder if Kant's criticism is valid against such bold scepticism of theoretical reason.

Kant denied the metaphysics of theoretical reason in order to guard religion and morality from attacks of reckless doubt. But religious belief could only maintain itself at the cost of Reason's being deprived of the power to establish a grand system of metaphysics. Even if we admit the existence of God and immortal spirit, they cannot be recognized by their attributes or functions. Such an existence is nothing more than a non-existence. Such knowledge is nothing more than ignorance.

[1] *K.r.V.*, B. p. 856, W.W. III, p. 536. *Prol.* para. 60, W.W. IV, p. 363. *K.p.V.*, I. I. 2., W.W., V, p. 71.
[2] Hegel, *Gesch. d. Ph.*, 2nd. edn., p. 538.
[3] *K.r.V.*, B. p. 623, W.W. III, p. 399.

Kant thought it necessary to restrict speculative reason [1] because otherwise it was led into transcendental dialectic [2] or transcendental illusion in its attempt to recognize trans-sensible objects. The forms of transcendental dialectic are firstly the paralogisms of rational psychology, which, from the universal form of consciousness "cogito," infer that the ego is a substance; secondly, four pairs of cosmological antinomies viz. the finitude versus the infinity of the world, simplicity versus complexity, natural causality versus causality from freedom, and the existence versus the non-existence of necessary being; and thirdly, the ideals of theology concerning the existence of God. Of these three kinds of transcendental illusion, the paralogisms and ideals do not involve any contradiction. They consist either in fallacious inferences or in unjustified assertions. But in the antinomy both thesis and antithesis may be proved independently; hence, taken together they necessarily result in a contradiction. For this reason Kant regarded the antinomy [3] as the most striking example of transcendental illusion.

In short, transcendental dialectic or transcendental illusion is either a fallacious inference or a violation of the law of contradiction committed by Reason when it infers in the same way as Understanding. Kant did not think of doubting whether this principle of logic was valid for Reason as well as for Understanding. He believed in the universal validity of this principle and used it as a criterion against which to judge speculative reason. But perhaps he should have been more prudent in his choice of criterion, especially in consideration of his famous distinction of Reason from Understanding. Suppose different criteria were appropriate to Understanding and Reason, what about the contradiction in the antinomy? Should it not be solved as the misapplication of criteria rather than as the break-down of Reason? Should we not assume the contradiction to prove the supremacy of speculative Reason over Understanding instead of giving up speculation and withdrawing to practical belief? This solution by no means tells against the point of transcendental philosophy, since the methods

[1] *K.r.V.*, tr. Dial, 2. B. 3. H. 7. Abs. B, p. 662, W.W. III, 422.
[2] Kant follows the ancient meaning of 'dialectic' as logic of illusion or as sophistic art. The illusion arises either in general logic or in transcendental logic. General logic is essentially the canon of knowledge. Dialectic arises when this logic is misused as an organon to produce objective assertions. In transcendental logic, we fall into dialectic, when our understanding makes synthetic judgements about objects in general over and above the limit of empirical use, in other words, when it is used trans-empirically. Kant applies the same word 'dialectic' both to dialectical illusions, and to the criticism of these illusions, but he admits himself that the latter is more properly called anti-dialectic. Cf. *K.r.V.*, tr. Log., Einl. III, W.W. III, pp. 79 ff.
[3] *Prol.* para. 50, W.W. IV, p. 338.

of mathematics, natural science, and metaphysics as the object of transcendental philosophy are not the same as the method which constitutes the transcendental philosophy itself. [1] Transcendental philosophy is neither the knowledge of understanding like mathematics and natural science, nor the practical belief or knowledge which Kant ascribed to metaphysics. It is, without doubt, an example of speculative knowledge of theoretical reason. Even the Kant who gave us the methods of science and metaphysics failed to reflect about the methodology of his own transcendental philosophy. This is indeed a good example of the finitude of human reason, which only comes to light through historical development.

The task of developing transcendental philosophy into a system of metaphysics instead of leaving it a mere criticism, and of restoring the metaphysics of speculative reason, was left to the philosophers of German Idealism, especially Hegel.

---

[1] Cf. Wundt, *op. cit.*, pp. 400 ff.

CHAPTER IV

METAPHYSICS AND DIALECTIC

I. HEGEL

The Critique of Pure Reason was characterized by Kant as ontology, the introductory part of metaphysics. The main part of ontology or transcendental philosophy was constituted by transcendental logic. Beside this newly-invented part of logic, Kant admitted general logic, [1] which is the same as formal logic and deals with the forms of thinking in general. Transcendental logic also abstracts the content of experience, but not, like general logic, all content of knowledge. While general logic deals with both empirical and pure knowledge, transcendental logic should be confined to the *a priori* knowledge of understanding and reason. It is a science which determines the objective validity of this knowledge. Combined with transcendental aesthetic, transcendental logic forms the *Critique of Pure Reason*. Hegel attached much importance to this transcendental logic and attempted to make it the substitute for 'previous metaphysics,' calling it an objective logic.

Kant did not develop his logic enough to cover metaphysics entirely. As was said above (Ch. III), transcendental logic, which was at first a criticism of metaphysics or a theory of knowledge, became in the later stage of the work itself a kind of metaphysics, though Kant himself did not acknowledge this explicitly. Transcendental logic, which was opposed both to formal logic and to transcendental aesthetic, did not cover the whole territory of knowledge. The separation of transcendental aesthetic and transcendental logic, together with the passivity of sensible intuition and the presupposition of the thing in itself, was the proof of the incomplete domination of transcendental logic over metaphysics.

This separateness of logic and metaphysics tended to disappear in Fichte and Schelling. Fichte did not require for knowledge any sensible data. He replaced Kant's opposition of theoretical reason and practical reason with the radical supremacy of practical reason. Thus, knowledge is no more a passive state of reason affected by the thing in itself; it is rather the self-determination of the ego, which sets up the non-

[1] Kant, *K.r.V.*, tr. *Log.*, Einl. II. W.W. IV, p. 82 f.

ego only for its performance of practical conduct. Schelling established
the self-identity of spirit and nature in place of the supremacy of
practical reason and ego. Kant's idea of the finite subject was
abandoned, and transcendental philosophy became itself metaphysics.

The philosophy of Fichte and Schelling, however, was a chain of
incomplete essays devoid of systematic coherence, so that the task
of reflecting on and evaluating metaphysics and logic was left to Hegel.
Hegel's solution to this problem consisted in subsuming formal logic
under transcendental logic and raising up the whole of logic from mere
theory of knowledge to metaphysics. [1] Hegel replaced metaphysics by
an objective logic, 'the science of the world that must be constructed
through thoughts.' [2] This objective logic includes, in addition to ontology or the science of being in general, the other parts of metaphysics
on mind, world and God, i.e. not only Kant's transcendental logic, but
also the whole scope of *metaphysica generalis* and *metaphysica specialis*.
Metaphysics before Kant was distinguished from this objective logic
in that it was based on 'representations' and neglected to criticize the
forms of thought. Kant's criticism, however, Hegel considers, confined
itself to the transcendental character of thinking, without going into
the investigation of thought-determinations themselves. This problem
remained for Hegel to solve himself with his 'objective logic.' [3] If,
however, as Hegel maintained, objective logic was to be a new science
which included the whole of metaphysics and was a substitute for
the old metaphysics, then Logic had to be regarded as wider than
metaphysics, for, besides metaphysics, it included subjective logic. [4]
According to Hegel's division of the science of logic, objective logic

[1] Hegel, *EL.* para. 24, W.W. Gk. VIII, p. 83. *WL.* Vor. W.W. IV, p. 16. The identification
of metaphysics with logic began already with Wolff. At the beginning of his logic, before the
analysis of the concept of being, he treated the principles of the first philosophy. These are
identity, contradiction, excluded middle, and sufficient reason. It may seem strange to us
who have made these principles the objects of logic to find them taken as principles of
being. But originally they were the priciples of being rather than thinking. For Aristotle's
logic was essentially ontological, and thinking was founded upon being. So Wolff's treatment
was traditional. But even here we can find a tendency to reduce ontology to logic. (Heimsoeth, *Studien*, etc. 7) This tendency advanced gradually in Baumgarten and in Kant. Kant
made metaphysics the object of logical criticism. Logic became predominant. Hegel proceeded
further and reduced metaphysics to logic. (cf. Hegel, *Über den Vortrag der philosophischen
Vorbereitungswissenschaften auf Gymnasien.* W.W. III, p. 306). Similarly with Fichte. His
Wissenschaftslehre treats these principles metaphysically, though in its literal sense 'Wissenschaftslehre' is the theory of knowledge or logic. On the other hand, even Hegel proceeded
to this end gradually. For we see in his early system, in the Jena period, that metaphysics
was independent of logic. In this period Hegel seems to have followed Wolff's tradition and
treated these principles in metaphysics.
[2] *WL.*, Einl. IV, p. 64.
[3] *Ibid.*, cf. EL. para. 41, W.W. VIII, pp. 123 ff.
[4] *EL.*, Einl., W.W. IV, p. 53.

is the science of being and essence, while subjective logic is the science of the concept. [1] It is because he subsumes metaphysics under logic that he calls the first part of his system logic instead of metaphysics or ontology. This corresponds to the fact that Hegel's system belongs to the line of idealism, which presupposes the concept as the ground of being, in opposition to the line of realism, which admits being as the foundation of concepts.

Neither the friends nor the enemies of metaphysics would object to Hegel's remark that the *former* metaphysics was routed by Kant's *Critique of Pure Reason*. [2] But what is then the so-called *former* [3] metaphysics? We must bear in mind that it particularly refers to the special theory of Wolff's school, and not to every theory in the history of metaphysics nor to metaphysics as a *branch* of *philosophical* science. Hence Hegel attacks, [4] without any inconsistency, the popular philosophers who mistook Kant's theory to imply absolute denial of metaphysics.

Hegel does not object to former metaphysics because it was concerned with intelligible objects like the mind, the world, and God. The chief fault of that metaphysics, on Hegel's view, [5] is that it presupposed ready-made subjects formed from mere representations of the complete beings, and attributed to them the determinations of understanding. According to Hegel, the thinking of mere understanding is essentially finite and sticks to finite determinations. When metaphysics is constructed by this kind of thinking, it must fall into one-sided dogmatism [6] as the result of its conviction that one of two opposite attributes must be negated if the other is to be affirmed of one subject. Thinking about metaphysical objects should be, Hegel maintains, the infinite thinking of reason, which, unlike the thinking of mere understanding, involves in itself opposite determinations in harmony. Such real metaphysics is called by Hegel idealism of speculative philosophy. [7] "In contrast to dogmatic metaphysics, which sticks to one-sided determination of thought in its isolation, the idealism of speculative philosophy is founded upon the principle of the whole, and

---

[1] *WL.*, Einl., W.W. IV, p. 65.

[2] *WL.*, Vorr., W.W. IV, p. 13.

[3] Sometimes it is called *alte Metaphysik*, but *alte Metaphysik* or *ältere Metaphysik* may have the wider meaning of metaphysical theories in general. Cf. *WL.*, W.W. IV, p. 39. *EL.*, para. 28. *Zus.* W.W. VIII, pp. 100 ff. etc.

[4] *WL.*, Vor. I. W.W. IV, p. 14; *G. Ph.*, W.W. XIX, p. 609.

[5] *EL.*, para 30. W.W. VIII, p. 104.

[6] *Ibid.*, para. 32. p. 105.

[7] *Ibid.*, para. 32. *Zus.*, para. 36, *Zus.* pp. 106, 115.

manifests itself as covering the onesided abstract determinations of understanding." For example the metaphysics of understanding required the mind to be determined as either finite or infinite, and when this requirement was not met it fell into paradox and was broken up. To the idealism of speculative philosophy on the contrary, the mind is neither merely finite nor merely infinite; in one sense, it is both, and in another sense it is neither. Neither determination has value in separation from the other: they must be applied as *moments* of an enhanced (*aufgegebene*) whole. The former metaphysics committed the fault of attempting to recognize infinite or absolute being with understanding which depends upon the law of contradiction. Kant's transcendental logic has the merit [1] of pointing out the inevitable paradox brought about by this unsuitable method of acquiring knowledge. But Hegel assumes it to be a fatal error on Kant's part that he laid the responsibility for this paradox on the impotence of theoretical reason, and, instead of setting up a real speculative metaphysics, made room for faith. In consideration of this point, Hegel intends to reconstruct a metaphysics which recognizes absolute being through the speculation of dialectical reason transcending the law of contradiction.

In place of the name 'metaphysics,' Hegel preferred, perhaps not without reason, the more informative expression 'idealism of speculative philosophy.' Here is, however, the origin of an interpretation that opposes dialectic to metaphysics or takes dialectic in separation from speculative thinking. The subject of our next pursuit, therefore, should be the investigation of the way in which Hegel's dialectic is related to speculative thinking.

Hegel distinguishes three sides or rather aspects of the logical.[2] These are not the same as the parts of logic mentioned above, i.e. the objective and the subjective, the one corresponding to being and essence, the other to the concept. They are in fact the moments of 'concept' or 'everything that is true.' The first aspect is abstract and is related to understanding, the second dialectical or negatively rational, and the third speculative or positively rational.

Now, the first side or aspect, i.e. the abstract, insists upon fixed determinations of objects and their difference from each other. The advantage and merit of this thinking of the understanding, Hegel admits, must not be ignored, for it gives determinations to both theory

[1] *Ibid.*, para. 48, pp. 139 ff.
[2] *Ibid.*, para. 79, p. 184.

and practice, and is 'suitable to the grace of God,' 'a necessary condition essential to the perfection of objects.' [1] Yet this kind of thinking
falls, as mentioned above, into dogmatism and into paradox through
its insistence upon one-sided determinations. The dialectical moment, [2]
as the second aspect, is the negation of finite determinations essential
to understanding, and the transition towards the opposite determinations. This paradox, seen from the side of understanding, leads to
scepticism, which Hegel divides into two types. First, the ancient noble
scepticism represented, for example, by Sextus Empiricus. Disappoint-
ed with the claims of understanding, it retires undisturbed and self-
confident. Second, the modern pre- and post-critical scepticism. It
denies the truth and certainty of supersensible being, and relies on the
evidence of the senses. Scepticism is generally considered to be an un-
conquerable enemy of knowledge, but according to Hegel it only denies
the finite and abstract thinking of understanding, and is in fact a
dialectical *moment* of philosophy. But philosophy is, of course, re-
luctant to remain in this negative state of scepticism. In a negative
state, there is actually something positive involved as a moment. The
recovery of the positive through the negative, (that is, the third aspect)
is called the speculative or the positively rational. [3] This last type of
thinking apprehends the unity of opposite determinations, the positive
that manifests itself in the dissolution and transition of phenomena.
In German, *Spekulation* usually means commercial adventure. But
even in this everyday use of the word, there is implied the requirement
that the subjective must be realized in the objective existence. In its
strictly philosophical usage, speculation means thinking, not mere
subjective thinking, thinking which manifests itself as a whole, holding
in harmony the opposites that could not be mastered by understanding.
What is speculative cannot be described by one-sided propositions.
It is the same as what is called mystic. Though it seems to be absolutely secret and incomprehensible, it is really so only for understanding
and by no means completely transcends every kind of thinking. It comprises opposite and fixed determinations of understanding as a re-
conciled unity, and can well be elucidated by rational thinking.

The comparison of Hegel's three aspects of the logical with Kant's
three stages [4] of metaphysics would, I think, be a useful way of explaining their different conceptions of metaphysics. Kant's stages of

[1] *Ibid.*, para. 80, *Zus.* 186.
[2] *Ibid.*, para. 81, pp. 189 ff.
[3] *Ibid.*, pp. 82. 195 ff.
[4] Kant, *Fortsch.*, W.W. VIII, p. 240 f. Cf. Ch. IV, para. 5.

metaphysics were (1) theorétical-dogmatic progress, (2) sceptical halt, and (3) practical-dogmatic completion. The correspondence between the two kinds of division is quite evident. Kant's theoretical-dogmatic progress corresponds to the abstract or intellectual in Hegel, the sceptical halt in Kant to the dialectical or negatively rational in Hegel, and practical dogmatic completion in Kant to the speculative or positively rational by Hegel. Both philosophers call the first stage *dogmatic* and the second stage *sceptical*. Only the third stage seems, at first sight, to be somewhat different for the two. But looking at it more closely, what Kant calls dogmatic implies rather what is positive than what is one-sided as Hegel meant, so that the only difference between them consists in the point that what was considered by Kant as positive in practical reference exclusively, became in Hegel speculatively positive as well. The word 'speculative' was also used by Kant to mean theoretical knowledge especially of concepts or objects beyond the range of mere experience. The comparison of these lists shows us, therefore, that the ideas of the absolute, which were in a special way admitted by Kant only to practical reason, were openly given by Hegel as subject matter to theoretical reason. This difference is quite conformable with Hegel's criticism of Kant's philosophy to the effect that it was nothing more than a philosophy of understanding. [1]

The distinction between understanding and reason, the one as the thinking faculty that determines objects through finite and fixed concepts founded upon the law of contradiction, the other as that which applies infinite concepts of totality to absolute being, originates, as Hegel admits, from Kant. [2] Hegel's divergence, or, one may say, his development from Kant consists in attributing theoretical cognition to this Reason. How then are dialectic, speculative logic, and mysticism related to each other? We learned that dialectic was qualified by Hegel as negatively rational, and speculative thinking as positively rational. Dialectic or negatively rational thinking is situated between the abstract – that which pertains to understanding – and the speculative: it is the intermediate stage through which the abstract thinking of the understanding ascends to speculative rational thinking, the negative moment through which the finiteness of the understanding reveals its latent contradictions and is broken up. Seen from the standpoint of the understanding, this negation or the breaking up of this thinking is taken as the bare abandonment of cognition, which must

[1] G. Ph., W.W. XIX p. 610. Cf. EL. para. 52. Zus. W.W. VIII, p. 151
[2] Ibid., p. 574.

inevitably lead to scepticism. One who would not like to admit any theoretical thinking other than that of understanding might find no other way than to give up all knowledge whatsoever and find his refuge in faith or in mysticism. It seems to me that Hegel inclined to assume Kant himself to be a repudiator of metaphysics like his followers. Whether this view is right or wrong, we may dismiss for the moment. But so far as theoretical reason is concerned, it was really Kant's own conclusion. The dialectic was regarded by Kant as a sign of the impossibility of metaphysics, for the law of contradiction was, for Kant, not only the principle of finite abstract thinking by the understanding, but also the principle of thinking in general, and consequently, of reason as well. Now Hegel agrees with Kant that dialectic should be the logic of negative reason. In other words, reason is merely negative as far as it remains in the stage of dialectic. So that theoretical reason may complete metaphysics as a systematic knowledge of absolute being, it must ascend to speculative thinking which is positively rational. It is of course something higher than the mere understanding, but the positive character is common to both. This speculative thinking, as the positively rational, is thought by Hegel to resemble the mystical. A remarkable utterance indeed, deserving of serious attention. Does it suggest that speculative logic is really a mystical method and that speculative metaphysics should be mysticism? If this is not so and the logic of this positive reason could also be called dialectic, should we not then admit two kinds of dialectic, the negative and the positive?

The dialectic is the logic of negative reason, it signifies the failure of the understanding in its attempt to conceive absolute being with finite determinations. Whereas speculation is the function of positive reason, in which every contradiction is enhanced. Taking these two statements separately, it seems almost possible to interpret the dialectic as merely showing us the finite power of the understanding, and speculation is entitled to understand the matter without any contradiction: there is, in reality, no contradiction at all. But this, I say, is a misinterpretation of Hegel's thought. It is true that what falls into paradox in the attempt to know the absolute is Understanding. But it is Reason's task to acknowledge the fatal contradiction that Understanding must encounter. So far, so good. Transcendental idealism, however, remained here, and could not proceed to acknowledge a positive task for critical reason. To Hegel's regret, transcendental idealism led to the mean conclusion of admitting the supremacy of practical reason.

Against this Hegel's mission was to bestow on Reason the speculative knowledge of the absolute.

This speculative reason arises from the insight of the necessity of dialectic – a logic of contradiction. It apprehends the unity of opposites, not unity without opposition. The immediate intuition of an integral whole would be mystical enlightenment akin to sensible evidence or faith, not conceptual knowledge, and therefore not philosophical. The difference between speculation and mystical experience is that the former presupposes dialectic and embraces in itself contradiction fused and elevated to a harmonious whole. "Dialectic movement alone is really speculative, and the declaration of this movement alone is speculative expressions." [1] "The dialectical principle is the soul of real scientific knowledge." [2] These propositions of Hegel show clearly the paradoxical truth that the essence of speculative or positively rational cognition consists in the self-conscious pursuit of dialectical or negatively rational cognition. Thus we might say that Hegel actually admitted dialectic as the method of metaphysics, though he followed Kant in regarding dialectic as negatively rational. The substantial content of speculative philosophy therefore might well be admitted to be dialectic. The dialectic which was once the revelation of Reason's inability grew more potent, and became the actual form in which Reason reflected on itself, and, furthermore, it came to be qualified as the form of reality, truth, and concept – which are all genuine objects of reason. "Every movement, every life, and every activity in reality is dialectic." [3] In this proud assertion of Hegel's, we find a germ of thought which will grow into the theory of the Marxists, who regard dialectic as the law of being rather than as a mere law of thinking, giving the function of active Reason to dialectic instead of to speculation, and thus forming a metaphysics out of dialectic. What should be borne in mind, however, I think, is that, in Hegel, dialectic could be the form of Reality as far as that Reality was constituted by concepts. I cannot therefore understand how Marxists, with their contention that mere being, i.e. being independent of understanding or consciousness, should be dialectic, and with their assumption that dialectical thinking should be the faithful copy of that being, could pretend to prove successfully that such a being is immediately dialectical by itself. Dialectical should not be a mere appearance of

---

[1] *Phän.* Vor., W.W. II, p. 59.
[2] *EL.* para. 81. *Zus.* 1., W.W. VIII, p. 190.
[3] *Ibid.*

incomplete thinking, by understanding, which is unable to attain the truth of being, it should rather be a moment necessary for speculative thinking, in the sense, namely, that Reason should be mediated by the breakdown of Understanding, when it should actually recognize absolute being. So far, we have no quarrel with the Marxists. But I feel sure it must follow of necessity from this very determination of dialectic that it can no more be a phenomenon of mere being apart from thinking. Materialism, which lost sight of this other side of 'dialectic,' made the mistake of taking dialectic undialectically. The opposition and its intercession (*Aufhebung*) can no more be an attribute or function of mere being than it can be the function of mere thinking, to say nothing of sheer matter. Matter is nothing but a moment of being or its phenomenal form. The attributes of matter or being are coordinate, their appearances succeed or are juxtaposed with one another: there is neither real contradiction nor its intercession. Contradiction is a phenomenon of peculiarly logical character. It presupposes Understanding. Only through contact with Understanding can contradiction be attributed to being or to matter. In the being before and apart from Understanding, everything is undifferentiated or rather it is in chaos. As mentioned above, Hegel called his new metaphysics idealism of speculative philosophy. In his system dialectic was necessary as the negative moment of speculative logic. At least, it was possible by presupposing the correspondence of Reason to being. How is it, then, possible for materialism, which admits mere matter as metaphysical substance, to succeed into the marvellous heritage of speculative idealism, "dialectic?"

2. ENGELS

In Hegel, metaphysics must be the system of speculative thinking; it must be an idealism and requires dialectic as its necessary moment. The Marxists' view of metaphysics and dialectic is quite different from this. Marxism is an eclecticism formed by combining Hegel's dialectic and Feuerbach's materialism. Feuerbach's neglect of Hegel's dialectic is not, I think, unreasonable. The reader who is acquainted with my view in the preceding section will not demand a further elucidation of this view. But Marxists are brimful of confidence in their dialectical development. Not only was idealism converted to materialism, but the relations between metaphysics and dialectic changed from friendliness to hostility. It is the orthodox theory of contemporary Marxism to oppose dialectic to metaphysics. This school, however, which more than others is inclined to dogmatism, completely neglects the analysis and investigation of the origins of its special terminology.

The line of thought, so worthy of attention, that opposes dialectic to metaphysics, admitting the former as the right way of acquiring knowledge, rejecting the latter as erroneous, originates from Engels. According to him, metaphysics is the theory which regards being as a mere aggregate of independent objects separated from each other, views Nature as fixed and unmovable states, denies its development, and assumes it to be mere repetition of this same process. Whilst dialectic is, on the contrary, the method of acquiring knowledge, which regards being as a whole, as a system of dynamic development. How on earth did he come by such an ingenious idea? By what interpretation of history did Engels come to confine metaphysics, which is properly a branch of philosophy, to such a peculiar theory? In his principal work, *Herrn Eugen Dührings Umwälzung der Wissenschaft*, [1] conventionally called *Anti-Dühring*, he states that the philosophers in ancient Greece were dialecticians by nature, especially Aristotle, a man of most profound scholarship, who was already studying the essential forms of dialectical thinking. But in modern philosophy, Engels considers, although dialectic had found brilliant exponents in Descartes and Spinoza, it fell into the so-called metaphysical way of thinking mainly through the influence of English thought. The French thinkers of the 18th century were, at least in their specifically philosophical works, almost entirely under the yoke of this metaphysical way of thinking.

I am afraid that this historical summary resembles a paper by an inferior student. How are we to understand a concept of dialectic that covers the whole of Greek philosophy? It is true that Aristotle studied the forms of dialectic. But even those with a very rudimentary acquaintance with the history of philosophy know how Aristotle depreciated that way of thinking. As for the idea of a modern dialectic, represented by Descartes and Spinoza, we can only wonder if by some chance the word 'dialectic' was misprinted in place of 'metaphysics.'

The authentic history of philosophy shows us that Greek philosophers were *metaphysicians* by nature, that modern *metaphysics* found its most brilliant exponents in Descartes and Spinoza, and that English empiricists *denied* this *metaphysics* introducing positivistic

[1] Einl. p. 22. Dietz.

ways of thinking into philosophy. It is generally accepted too that anti-metaphysical thinking became prevalent in France in the 18th century. In the *Holy Family*, [1] Marx, the esteemed friend of Engels, used the word 'metaphysics' in accordance with this authentic interpretation of history. He gave the following examples of metaphysicians: Descartes, Malebranche, Spinoza, and Leibniz; and of anti-metaphysicians: Gassendi, F. Bacon, Locke, Hobbes, Condillac, Voltaire, Bayle, etc. According to Marx, the metaphysics of the 17th century was eclipsed by the philosophy of the Enlightenment, especially by French 18th century materialism, and afterwards restored by German speculative philosophy of the 19th century. Hegel was a champion of this speculative metaphysics, and founded a universal kingdom of metaphysics. This metaphysics, so Marx argued, was again denied by Feuerbach. Marx's description is quite in accordance with orthodox terminology, and there is no trace to be found in it of the capricious idea that opposes metaphysics to dialectic.

Hegel restored metaphysics by setting up a speculative philosophy with the mediation of dialectic. This is a generally accepted idea – accepted even by Marx. But, in spite of this, Engels ventures to upset the 'vulgar' opinion. Dialectic should be the radical opposite of metaphysics. It is, I repeat, an original idea peculiar to Engels, so not strictly to be called Marxism. No wonder, it is only suitable for a revolutionary thinker to upset traditional theory, if only it could be succesfully verified by the analysis of history! Let us then consider Engels' reasons for making this statement as an investigation of the grounds of his revolutionary theory.

Engels points out firstly [2] that the phenomena which appear to our naive observation are relations and mutual operations infinitely confused; everything appears to be moving, changing and shifting. Now, he thinks, the right way of understanding the world can be found in the ancient Greek philosophers, especially in Heraclitus, who maintained that everything *is* and *is not* at the same time, because everything is for ever shifting. Indeed, Heraclitus' theory involves an idea similar to the Hegelian dialectic. This was in fact what Hegel pointed out when he expounded his theory of dialectic. But what about Parmenides? Was he not an ancient Greek philosopher – no less important than Heraclitus? To neglect this prominent and famous opposition and to decide that the ancient Greek philosophers were

---

[1] *Die Heilige Familie*, pp. 253 ff. Dietz.
[2] *Anti-Dühring*, pp. 22 ff.

in general attached to the theory of constant motion, is a prejudiced opinion – in Engels' way of speaking, a quite "metaphysical and un-dialectical dogma." If one wishes to call ancient Greek philosophy in general dialectic, one should speak of the history of Greek philosophy rather than of a theory of this or that particular philosopher. For inasmuch as dialectic is the logic of development, one may find dialectic wherever there is rigorous thinking.

In what way, then, did Engels explain the development of what he considers to be metaphysics? He said the philosophy of the ancient Greeks (whom he called dialecticians by nature!) could not explain individual phenomena, though they understood the general character of the whole. So there arose a need to investigate the nature and causality of these individual phenomena in separation from their natural or historical situations. This, the abstract analysis of phenomena, was the subject of Natural Science and historical research. Since, however, he continues, such a study requires the collection of materials, it remained undeveloped in Greece. Scholars of the Alexandrian Period and mediaeval Arabians engaged in the strict research of nature; but it was only in the second half of the 19th century that natural science in the proper sense had made rapid progress. The great development during the last 400 years was the study of nature by analysing it into individual parts, dividing various processes and appearances into definite classes, and investigating the inside of an organism by dissection. So far, there is certainly no objection to be made. However, Engels goes on to say that a tendency developed to analyse nature into immobile, unchangeable, fixed, and lifeless states separated from the whole, and once this analytical intellectual (verständige) method of science was applied to philosophy, there began "the prejudice peculiar to several recent centuries, viz., the metaphysical way of thinking." In his opinion, it was Bacon and Locke who introduced this analytical method of science into philosophy. In succession to this comes the famous sentence, repeated a million times by faithful Marxists, "For a metaphysician, both things and their reflection in thinking, viz. concepts, are to be regarded as separate independently observable, fixed, stiff objects given at a stroke."[1]

We understand by this that what Engels meant by the word 'metaphysics' is neither the theory of being nor theology, nor even the dogmatic and deductive way of thinking, but rather the way of thinking that results from applying the analytical method of modern natural

[1] *Ibid.*, p. 24.

science to philosophy. For the moment, he does not go so far as to assume that modern science is metaphysical. But it is a remarkable and rather astounding judgement of Engels that the origin of the metaphysical way of thinking was to be found *in modern science*, instead of in ancient philosophy or mediaeval theology. From his statements, it seems as if one might infer without the possibility of falsification that the dialectic, which he recommends to us as the true method of philosophy, was going strong in that unscientific speculation of ancient philosophy, and was replaced by the analytical method of modern natural science. I don't know how this could be called a progressive theory.

But, joking apart, let us take his words in a more favourable sense. Even if we do this, Engels' words amount to the assertion that the analytical thinking of modern natural science cannot be employed in philosophy. Dialectic, as the true method of philosophy, is not a scientific analytical way of thinking, but rather the seeing of things as a whole ... say, speculative. However, a devoted communist of non-philosophical temperament who is deep in a text book might be offended at my interpretation.

Now, among present-day Marxists, Dialectical Materialism is generally considered to be compatible with the view of common sense, to which metaphysics or idealism is opposed. With this in mind, they mock the crazy idealists who deny the existence of the world before the origin of mankind. Unfortunately for the Marxists, we find that Engels immediately after making the statement quoted above explains that it is the analytical and consequently metaphysical view which is faithful to common sense; whilst dialectic both contradicts and goes beyond *vulgar* opinion. Metaphysical thinking, he says, which considers that a thing either exists or does not exist, that it is impossible for anything to be itself and something else at the same time, that the positive and the negative exclude one another, that cause and effect oppose each other as fixed terms, this metaphysical thinking agrees with common sense and appears at first sight to be right. But, looking at it more closely, we see that it is by no means a correct view of reality. ... Things and their reflection in concepts should be held essentially in their reference, connexion, movement, coming to be and passing away, and these processes are the proof of the correctness of this way of thinking ... Nature is the touchstone of dialectic; it presents a lot of evidence to prove, against the view of modern natural science, that it is in the last resort not metaphysical but dialectical.

As an example of this new point of view, Engels mentions Darwinism and assumes that recent German philosophy used the dialectical method in the development theory stemming from the Kant-Laplace theory and brought to completion in Hegel's system. [1] From this statement we know that what Engels meant by 'metaphysics' was the method of natural science in the 18th century, which originated with the English empiricists, whereas dialectic was the orthodox method of German philosophy. [2] Just as in the case of Aristotle, here also Kant's negative estimation of dialectic is completely neglected. But it is commonly accepted that German philosophy is the legitimate successor of metaphysics, and even in the case of Kant, who appears to be an exception, his interest was, as we argued above (Ch. III), mainly directed to the reconstruction of metaphysics. Marx himself was of our opinion: he actually admitted that Hegel's system was the completion of speculative metaphysics. To Engels, however, Kant and Hegel appeared to have been dialecticians in the tradition of Descartes and Spinoza. Through what profound speculation did Engels really come to this new supposition, against common sense, and even against Marx?

We notice that Engels' concept of metaphysics is akin in its content to the way of thinking by the understanding as is explained by Hegel. According to Hegel, understanding is the faculty of empirical knowledge and unsuitable for philosophy, which is essentially the knowledge of intelligible being as a whole. He considered that this misemployment of scientific method in philosophy was the cause of dialectic, viz. of negatively rational logic. The example of this false theory was to be found in the so-called former metaphysics, especially the metaphysics of the understanding of Wolff's school. Kant's merit consisted in pointing out the unavoidable paradox to which this metaphysical theory must lead. Understanding may attain correct scientific knowledge insofar as it is applied to sensible data and operates as the thinking of empirical objects. What is condemned by a positivist like Comte is the system of a transcendent pure speculative inference. Comte called Kant the greatest metaphysician. But, in fact, Kant was of the same opinion in that he demanded the restraint of speculation. The man deservedly called the greatest metaphysician was Hegel rather than Kant. We must take into account, however, the fact that Hegel was a metaphysician not because he was undialectical – it was

[1] *Ibid.*, p. 26.
[2] *Ibid.*, p. 413 f. 'Alte Vorrede.'

Hegel himself who set up dialectic as the logic of metaphysics – but because he was speculative, unscientific, and because his logic was beyond the reach of understanding. It seems to me therefore to be very queer that Engels, who admired Hegel for setting up the dialectical method, entirely ignored the fact that it was just the same Hegel who completed speculative metaphysics. Perhaps this neglect is what Engels pretends to be a dialectical cancellation (*Aufheben*). Engel's disapproval of Hegel was confined to his idealism, and once this idealism was 'turned the right way up' there was no danger of speculation becoming metaphysics. [1] But what significance was there in Hegel's dialectic but for the restoration of metaphysics? [2] It would be an astonishing idea indeed for metaphysics to be supported by understanding, and scientific knowledge yielded by dialectic!

Now, Engels says, the dialectical tradition of German philosophy was succeeded by modern materialism. But, I am sorry, I can hardly find even a qualified example of modern materialism other than that of Engels himself. For all the other materialistic philosophers, such as Feuerbach, Vogt, Büchner, Moleschott or Häckel, were either severely criticised as undialectical or despised as vulgar. The scope of the concept 'modern' is also ambiguous, though this ambiguity is widespread and not peculiar to Engels. Anyhow, this modern materialism is, according to Engels, essentially dialectical, and there remains no need of a philosophy beside and beyond the special sciences. As soon as the requirement appears within each science to make clear its position in the framework of things and knowledge of Reality, a special science of this framework becomes unnecessary, and of all philosophical disciplines in the past, only the doctrine of thought and its rule remains, viz. formal logic and dialectic, the others being absorbed into the positive sciences of nature and history. [3] In this famous prediction Engels' thought becomes more and more confused. Why in the world does a special science of the framework become unnecessary, when reflection on the situation of a science appears within that science itself? Does this statement mean that the situation of a science

1 *Ibid.*, p. 28.
2 Hegel, *EL.* para. 98. *Zus.* W.W. VIII, p. 232.
"Only animals are actually pure physicists. For animals do not think. On the contrary, man, as the thinking being, is naturally a metaphysician. What must come into question is whether the metaphysics one employs is of the right kind or not, and whether or not one depends on the thought fixed by Understanding instead of concrete logical ideas." Let us call to mind the fact that a nation without metaphysics was compared by Hegel to a temple without God, and that the suspected denigration of metaphysics by Kant and Jacobi was condemned as philosophy without philosophy.
3 *Anti-Dühring*, p. 29

may be determined by itself without the aid of any theory of knowledge? But reflection on the framework of things and thought is quite different from any of the special sciences. Is dialectic as well as formal logic the science of knowledge, or is the science of knowledge confined to formal logic? If dialectic is something more than the science of knowledge, say, the science of the development of being, why is it not a science beyond the special sciences? Why should it not be called metaphysics or ontology? What is meant by 'everything other than formal logic and dialectic,' the pseudo-knowledge, formerly regarded as philosophy, but now to be resolved into the positive sciences of nature and history? Does Engels mean only the metaphysical theories before Kant or does he mean every philosophical discipline before himself? Further, if dialectic is also the science of thought, and if it alone can survive the demise of other philosophical disciplines, what difference is there between Engels and the Neo-Kantians who maintained that the only possible form of philosophy was the theory of knowledge? Besides, what is the relation between formal logic and dialectic, and what is the connection between these two kinds of logic and the method of the positive sciences? Is dialectic the dialectical way of thinking, or scientific reflection upon this way of thinking, or is it rather the law of being? As dialectic is called 'the science of general rules concerning the movement and development of nature, society and thinking,' [1] it seems as if it means the reflective consciousness of the law of movement and development, which rules over all Reality and thinking. It is thus epistemology and ontology, no different from Kant's transcendental philosophy or Hegel's objective logic. It is just the same as metaphysics in the proper sense. But if dialectic is thus admitted to be epistemology and ontology at the same time, what are the so-called positive sciences? And if dialectic is not the science of the law of movement and development in nature and society, what sort of knowledge is it? If dialectic exists beside the positive sciences, what is the method of the positive sciences, and how is it ruled by dialectic? What, in short, does the term 'positive science' mean? How is it distinguished from the method of modern analytical science since Bacon, i.e. what is called by Engels metaphysical thinking? It is regrettable that all these questions remain unanswered by Engels. We have found that Engels' concept of metaphysics has a quite particular meaning, a meaning which perhaps was unknown even to Marx. From whatever ignorance or mistake it may

---

[1] G. Ph., W.W. XIX, p. 439. "Locke's philosophy is, one would like to say, a metaphysics,', p. 423. "It is metaphysical empiricism." We may say the same thing with regard to Engels.

have arisen, now that Engels has become an authority for a great number of people we have no choice but to admit it as a special usage of the word 'metaphysics.' It indicates a view of the world through the abstract analytical thinking of understanding, a view which denies motion and change. It is the result of a misapplication of scientific method to philosophy, by Bacon, Locke and Wolff, and finds its representatives in French philosophy of the eighteenth century.

What is the origin of this peculiar view of metaphysics? It may be that Engels mistook what Hegel called former metaphysics, – i.e. those metaphysical theories which fell into paradox through attempting to cognise absolute being by means of understanding – for metaphysics in general, hastily overlooking the qualifications 'former' and 'of understanding.' Hegel himself has no positive responsibility for this confusion. He often severely criticized the metaphysics of the understanding, but was always explicit in qualifying it as 'former,' 'older,' or 'of the understanding.'[1] But if Hegel has any (negative) responsibility it is, in the first place, the fact that he called his new metaphysics idealism of speculative philosophy, instead of explicitly calling it speculative metaphysics or dialectical metaphysics. Presumably Hegel preferred this expression because in his complete system metaphysics is subsumed under logic and loses its independence.[2] But the subsumption of metaphysics under logic must not be confused with the opposition of metaphysics to (dialectical or speculative) logic. It must be emphasized moreover that metaphysics can be dissolved into logic only in idealism, which identifies concepts with reality, and not in materialism, which regards reality as of material character. Consequently materialism must subordinate logic to metaphysics.

Now, the second way in which Hegel is (negatively) responsible for this confusion is that he used a single word 'metaphysics' to mean both metaphysics as a branch of philosophy and a particular theory of metaphysics. Strictly speaking, we must distinguish metaphysics from metaphysical theories as well as from theories of metaphysics. The first is a branch of philosophy, the second, its special instances, and the third consists in reflections on metaphysics like Kant's *Critique of Pure Reason* and our present inquiry. The ambiguity of this expres-

[1] The only exception is *WL*. W.W. IV, p. 139. But in this place also it denotes in reality old metaphysics. As to Hegel's identification of Kant's philosophy with the metaphysics of Understanding, cf. *G. Ph.*, W.W. XIC, p. 570.

[2] *WL.*, Vorr. I. W.W. IV, p. 16. "...die logische Wissenschaft, welche die eigentliche Metaphysik oder reine spekulative Philosophie ausmacht." *EL*. Einl. para. 9. W.W. VIII, p. 53. "Die spekulative Logik enthält die vorige Logik und Metaphysik."

sion of Hegel's is, however, common to German authors, and not his
individual fault. Needless to say, Hegel could not make such a dis-
graceful mistake as to call Descartes or Spinoza dialecticians, or to
make Bacon the founder of metaphysical thinking. Hegel talks of the
empirical and positivistic thought of Bacon and Locke with a tone
of deep scorn, without concealing his nationalistic prejudice against
them. He admits that there may be found a kind of metaphysics in
Locke. [1] But the context shows explicitly enough that his intention was
far from that of Engels, who attributed a metaphysical way of thinking
to these empirical thinkers. So as to assess Engels' criticism of Bacon,
we must go back and examine Bacon's view of metaphysics.

Bacon [2] divided knowledge into Divinity and Philosophy. The one
descends from above, the other springs from beneath. The one is in-
spired by divine revelation, the other is informed by the light of nature.
In philosophy, a man's contemplation either penetrates as far as God
or is diverted to nature, or reflected back to himself. Corresponding
to these enquiries, philosophy divides into three branches. Divine
Philosophy, Natural Philosophy, and Human Philosophy or Humanity.
These branches must be supported by a universal science, *Philosophia
Prima*, i.e. Primary or Summary Philosophy. The first part of this
Philosophia Prima deals with axioms common to each of the special
branches; for instance, "if equals be added to unequals, the whole will
be unequal," or "things that are equal to the same thing are equal to
one another." These axioms, which apply both in mathematics and
logic and are useful for the advancement of sciences, have not yet been
systematized by anyone, though they are used in a great variety of
arguments. The second part of the *Philosophia Prima* is concerned
with adventitious conditions of essences, which are called Transcen-
dentals. Examples of these concepts would be: much, little; like, unlike;
possible, impossible; likewise being and not-being, etc. [3]

The first special branch of philosophy is, as we have said, divine
philosophy or natural theology. The term 'divine' comes from its object
and 'natural' comes from the origin of this knowledge; it is the knowledge obtained by the light of nature, [4] viz. through human reason.
The second branch is natural philosophy, i.e. the knowledge of Nature.

---

[1] *Proficiency and Advancement of Learning, Divine and Human*, 1605, W.W. Spedding III.
De Dignitate et Augmentis Scientiarum (The Dignity and Advancement of Learning) 1623.
W.W. I. (IV).
   [2] *Dign.* III, 1 (W.W. i, pp. 539 ff.) *Prof.* III (W.W. pp. 346 ff)
   [3] *Dign.* III. 2. (W.W. 1, pp. 544 ff.) *Prof.* II (EE. III, p. 349).
   [4] *Dign.* III. 3. (W.W. I, pp. 547 ff.) *Prof.* II. (W.W. III, p. 351).

It is subdivided into the speculative and the operative; the former is the investigation of causes, and the latter is concerned with the production of effects. The part of natural philosophy which is speculative and theoretical, is divided into special physics and metaphysics. [1] Here we encounter the concepts of metaphysics which is really peculiar to Bacon. In using this old word in a different way from that in which it is commonly used, Bacon explains that he is willing to follow antiquity and retain the ancient term but with an altered sense. He compares this to the moderate and approved process of innovation in civil matters, in which, though the state of things is changed, yet the form of order is retained. There are indeed many examples of this conventional treatment of terminology in the history of philosophy. Engels is one example, and Bergson, whom we shall study later, is another. But, regrettably, such a change in the meaning of a term is the origin of much confusion of thought, and the historical study of philosophy is burdened with the troublesome task of putting this confusion in order. Here is one task for a linguistic philosophy which aims at making the meanings of terms quite explicit.

Now, metaphysics as a special part of natural philosophy is concerned of course with nature and with nothing else, but only with the most excellent part of nature. For, unlike physics which deals with what is inherent in matter, and therefore transitory, metaphysics is concerned with what is more abstract and fixed. [2] And furthermore, whilst physics supposes in nature only being, movement, and natural necessity, metaphysics supposes also a mind and idea. [3] Seeing that the special part of natural philosophy as opposed to metaphysics is called by Bacon special physics, we may safely infer that the new metaphysics is synonymous with general physics.

Natural philosophy was divided into the investigation of causes and the production of effects, and the former was characterized as theoretical. Now that the theoretical part of natural philosophy is to be divided into special physics and metaphysics, the difference between these two branches of theoretical philosophy must correspond to the difference between the types of cause which these sciences investigate. Here Bacon employs Aristotle's concept of four causes, and says that physics investigates and handles the material and efficient causes, metaphysics the formal and final. Material and efficient

[1] *Dign.* III. IV. (W.W. I; p. 353).
[2] *Ibid.*
[3] *Ibid.*

causes are regarded by Bacon as vague, variable, and inconstant. [1]

As to form, which is the first object of metaphysics, Bacon considers that Plato was right in maintaining it the true object of knowledge, but was wrong to consider forms as absolutely abstracted from matter, and it was this error which diverted him to those *theoretical* speculations with which all his natural philosophy was infected and polluted.

The forms of substance, according to Bacon, are so complex and complicated that either it is vain to inquire into them at all, or such inquiry as is possible should be put off for a time, and not entered upon until the forms of the more simple natures have been satisfactorily investigated and discovered.

"To inquire into the form of a lion, of an oak, of gold, nay even of water or air, is a vain pursuit; (it is quite the contrary) to inquire into the form of dense, rare, hot, cold, heavy, light, tangible, pneumatic, volatile, fixed, and the like." These 'forms of the first class' are like the letters of the alphabet, not many in number, and yet they make up the essences and forms of all substances. To inquire into these forms is the subject of metaphysics. Bacon finds this part of metaphysics to be deficient, but he believes that it is the "most excellent" in two respects. In the first place because it is a short-cut which follows the ways of experience, which is the duty and virtue of all knowledge. In the second place, because it gives men the power to gain the maximum of liberty, and allows them to use this power in the widest and most extensive spheres. "Physics carries men in narrow and restrained ways, imitating the ordinary flexuous courses of nature; but the ways of the wise are everywhere broad." "Physical causes give light and direction to new inventions in similar matter. But whoever knows any form, knows also the utmost possibility of superinducing that nature upon every variety of matter." [2]

The second part of metaphysics is the inquiry into final causes. According to Bacon, this part has not been missing but has merely been misplaced. For it was generally looked for in physics and not in metaphysics. This misplacement is not to be passed over as a mere misclassification, for it "has caused a notable deficience, and been a great misfortune to philosophy. For the handling of final causes in physics has driven away and overthrown the diligent inquiry into physical causes." [3] The point of Bacon's saying is neither to reject final causes

[1] *Ibid.* (I. pp. 565 ff. III. p. 355).
[2] *Ibid.* (I. pp. 568 ff. III, pp. 357 ff.)
[3] *Anti-Dühring*, p. 28.

nor to decline a speculative inquiry into them. The main point rather
is to prevent the ruin of physics that might be brought about through
the intrusion of final causes into physical research. So long as these
two kinds of cause and their inquiries remain in their own territories,
they are both admitted as valid. For instance, the cause "that the
hairs of the eyelids (are there) for a quickset and fence about the sight"
is compatible with the cause "that pilosity is incident to orifices of
moisture." "The one declares an intention, and the object of metaphysics, the other a consequence and pertains to physics." Bacon assures us that research into physical causes never withdraws a man
from God and Providence, but on the contrary that it leads a philosopher to the confirmation of God and Providence.

This is a summary of Bacon's arguments on knowledge, especially
on metaphysics. We admit that Bacon's usage of the concept of metaphysics is somewhat relevant to Engels' opposition of dialectic to
metaphysics. Should we then take Engels' denial of metaphysics to be
directed against Bacon's special usage, i.e. on physics general instead of
on traditional metaphysics? Or was Engels really attacking Bacon's
method as a whole? Let us then examine whether Bacon's metaphysics
was so peculiar and deserved Engels' strictures.

It is true that the distinction between metaphysics and first philosophy goes back to Bacon. But it was not necessarily either an original or an arbitrary idea. Traditional metaphysics and first philosophy
have not always had the same content. At least, ontology and theology
were heterogeneous elements in Aristotle's first philosophy, and philosophers since then have been engaged in trying either to distinguish
or to synthesize these heterogeneous elements. Bacon's arguments may
be regarded as one attempt to solve this historical problem. The idea
that *natural theology* forms the first part of special philosophy, and
metaphysics as a branch of *natural philosophy* the second part, anti-
cipates Wolff's classification of metaphysics, in which *metaphysica
specialis* is divided into natural theology, cosmology, and psychology;
Bacon's metaphysics partly corresponds to Wolff's cosmology. The
characterization of metaphysics as the inquiry into fixed forms and
final causes, especially the idea that metaphysics deals with abstract
and fixed form as opposed to physics which deals with material things
that change, might be thought relevant to Engels' accusation. But,
since this distinction may also be found in Aristotle, whom Engels
honoured with the title of dialectician, it would be unfair if Bacon were
to be blamed for making the same distinction. Moreover Bacon was

of the opinion that metaphysics is compatible with physics; he neither insisted that Nature was fixed and unchangeable, nor neglected the observation of concrete, moving things in the world.

It is true that the forms which he inquired into in his metaphysics were elementary attributes rather than the forms of substances. But he is to be praised for using this analytical method. He is quite right to contend that the forms of substances are difficult to investigate, and that they should be left until the abstracted elementary forms which constitute the form of substances become clear. To inquire without analysis into the forms of concrete substances such as the oak and the lion would result in the failures of Plato's theory of ideas, which only reduplicated the world of appearance. I doubt if Engels' dialectic, which has to perceive being as a whole, should be an inquiry concerning forms of substances like Plato's theory of ideas. Engels admitted, as we have said, that the unscientific speculation of the ancient Greeks, who were dialecticians by nature, could not explain individual phenomena. If such a speculation directed to being as a whole deserve the name of dialectic, it must be the same as mystical intuition, more primitive than the analytical logic of understanding, instead of a higher logic of reason. Dialectic really consists in the cancellation and fusion of contradictory oppositions. But there can be no real dialectical *Aufheben* without a previous opposition. A direct perception of being as a whole unmediated by the fixed determinations of understanding necessarily leads us to mysticism. We may call it a kind of speculation, but it is never dialectic. Furthermore, Bacon's metaphysics is a mere branch of natural philosophy, and nothing more. Of course we cannot find dialectic in Bacon, but we cannot judge his philosophy as a whole to be undialectical and metaphysical on the grounds that one particular branch of natural philosophy is mainly concerned with the analysis of forms.

Bacon's metaphysics is opposed to mechanical natural science, since it is concerned with the investigation of final causes. But Engels himself similarly rejects mechanical theory – calling it metaphysical – so that his criticism of Bacon does not touch on this point. Further, since Bacon admits the mechanical view to be compatible with the teleological view, we cannot assume his metaphysics to be one-sidedly teleological. Seeing that dialectic is considered even by Hegel to aim at the *Aufheben* of mechanical theory and teleology, it must be looked at as a development of Bacon's thought rather than running counter to it.

In short, Bacon's thoughts as a whole was by no means a one-sided dogmatism deserving of Engels' strictures. What must be acknowledged however is that Engels' special terminology in metaphysics is due to Bacon. There is no doubt that Engels' dialectic was set up against the special concept of metaphysics used by Bacon. Therefore the only theory against which Engels' criticism would be valid would be one which both retained Bacon's special concept of metaphysics and rejected the scientific or philosophical inquiries which he admitted alongside his metaphysics. Was there really any such philosophy? Were eighteenth century materialism or Wolff's system examples of it? Or should we take the undialectical materialism of the nineteenth century or, better, Eugen Dühring's philosophy as our example? To some extent all these would do. Yet the criticism of the defects of the abstract thinking of the understanding was the task begun by Kant and completed by Hegel, so Engels' unsatisfactory undertaking would be superfluous.

We must give Engels the credit of defending Hegel's dialectic at a time when it was rather unpopular. In fact, the chief point of his argument was the defence of dialectic; and the only trouble was that the concept of metaphysics was an unsuitable choice of antithesis. He would not have dreamed of criticizing metaphysics, if he had not had to do away with Mr. Dühring, who was a dangerous political enemy. Nowadays, all Engels' enemies – including Dühring – are for better or for worse buried in oblivion, and only Engels' criticism of metaphysics remains to commemorate their battles. It was due to this peculiar situation that Engels' criticism was diverted from its proper object and wrongly directed against traditional metaphysics or against any theory which might be advanced under the title of metaphysics. A tragicomedy, indeed. Engels does not bear the full responsibility. It is our misfortune that a book or, more exactly, a hasty piece of journalism survived its proper period of validity and gained imperishable fame, at least among a certain group of people.

At any rate, by recognizing Engels' special usage of the term 'metaphysics,' we find that Engels' argument is neither, as it is often mistakenly thought to be, a total denial of traditional metaphysical theories, nor a denial of metaphysics as a branch of philosophy or science. It is only a criticism of an undue emphasis put on a branch of natural philosophy first defined by Bacon, or, as one could say, an anti-thesis against French materialism, Wolff's metaphysical theory, and especially Dühring's theory. In other words, Engels' dialectical materialism, setting aside the question of its validity, is, at least in form, a kind of metaphysical theory, an instance of speculation belonging to the line of Greco-German tradition from Aristotle to Hegel. It is in this sense an antithesis against utilitarianism and abstract rationalism. And this conclusion may help us to understand something which perhaps even Marxists themselves are not aware of: that is, why they are so hostile towards logical positivism and analytical philosophy.

CHAPTER V

METAPHYSICS IN RECENT PHILOSOPHY

I. BERGSON

We might roughly characterise the ancient, mediaeval and modern eras as those of philosophy, religion and science respectively. If, as some progressive thinkers maintain, these were the stages through which the human mind developed, philosophy and religion would only have significance as mere remnants of past civilizations. Such a simple progressivism is certainly untenable, not only because it demolishes the multiformity of human culture, but also because it unconsciously contradicts itself by presupposing the idea of progress as a metaphysical dogma or religious belief. Philosophy, religion, and science are in fact forms of culture rather than stages of progress. Perhaps they are universal and eternal forms parallel to each other. What changes from period to period is only the comparative importance of a cultural form. We must admit that neither philosophy nor religion is dominant in our age, but it does not necessarily follow from this fact that we moderns may or must live without philosophy or religion. Of course ancient philosophy and mediaeval religion cannot be applied without any modification. They can secure their positions only through a *modus vivendi* with science, which is a favourite of the present time.

There are two ways in which present-day philosophy comes to terms with science. The one is by confining itself to the theory of knowledge or logic, giving up its claims in metaphysics and leaving such problems to science. The other is by making the theory of knowledge and logic mere parts of philosophy or its preliminary, and striving to establish an independent metaphysics. From this point of view, current philosophy may be divided into epistemological and metaphysical schools. Pragmatism, Logical Positivism, Analytical Philosophy, Logical Empiricism, Phenomenology, Neo-Kantianism, etc. belong to the first group, Existentialism, Philosophy of Life, and Neoscholasticism belong to the second. Marxism, as we have argued, belongs, as far as its explicit pronouncements go, to the first, but in reality, it belongs to the second. Our investigation will be confined to the remarkable attempts to rescue metaphysics by giving it a new meaning, for the fate of metaphysics mainly depends upon the success of these attempts.

There will perhaps be few objections if we choose Bergson and Heidegger as the representative defenders of metaphysics. There are of course many metaphysicians, great and small, besides these, for instance N. Hartman, A. N. Whitehead, and the Neoscholastic philosophers. But it seems to me that these metaphysicians do not take the predicament of metaphysics seriously enough, but instead stick to the old concept of metaphysics. At least they do not pretend to have invented a new concept of metaphysics.

According to Bergson, "A comparison of the definitions of metaphysics and the various conceptions of the absolute leads to the discovery that philosophers, in spite of their apparent divergencies, agree in distinguishing two profoundly different ways of knowing a thing. The first implies that we move round the object; the second that we enter into it. The first depends on the point of view at which we are placed and on the symbols by which we express ourselves. The second neither depends on a point of view nor relies on any symbol. The first kind of knowledge may be said to stop at the relative; the second, in those cases where it is possible, to attain the absolute." [1] I do not know what comparisons led Bergson to make this generalization. The conception itself shows some very personal traits of his. So that we might rather take it as an outline of his own thought.

Being a radical dualist in the French tradition since Descartes, Bergson maintained that intelligence and intuition were quite heterogeneous. The function of intelligence is analysis and interpretation by means of symbols, and this kind of knowledge constitutes positive science. The function of intuition is immediate sympathy with the object, and this is the method of metaphysics. [2] To go from intuition to analysis is easy, but the opposite direction is impossible. For this reason metaphysical knowledge is considered to be superior to and more profound than science. Bergson does not classify philosophy and science, for he has no interest in scholastic discriminations. Philosophy and metaphysics are roughly identified with one another and opposed to science. [3] Bergson says repeatedly that scientific knowledge is ruled by practical interest – and this is also the fundamental idea of William James' pragmatism. [4] What distinguishes Bergson from James is that he makes much of the disinterested knowledge of metaphysics whilst James sticks to pragmatic knowledge. Science is an instrument for

[1] Bergson, *La pensée et la mouvant.* VI. Introduction à la métaphysique, pp. 201 ff.
[2] *Ibid.*, p. 206.
[3] *Évolution créatrice*, p. 214.
[4] *Pensée.* pp. 225 f., 232, and 267 ff. *Évolution*, pp. 165 ff.

action, but philosophy or metaphysics is pure contemplation. [1] This
is not a new idea. The idea of dividing knowledge into theoretical and
practical, philosophy being theoretical, is classical, whereas that of
making practical knowledge the essence of science can be traced back
to Francis Bacon. What is peculiar to Bergson is only his special use
of the concepts of intuition and *intelligence* – best translated 'Understanding.' Intuition is the method of philosophy, intelligence the
method of science.

French philosophers generally do not distinguish Understanding
and Reason. This neglect of our heritage from ancient and mediaeval
times, to say nothing of Kant and Hegel, is a great disadvantage to
them. It may result in their making the notion of Understanding too
wide, so as to contain Reason. But in Bergson's case *intelligence* in
general has an extremely restricted role and cannot include intellectual
activities other than that of understanding. Besides understanding he
admits no faculty other than intuition, so that the intellectual activities
excluded from *intelligence* are forced into intuition. Bergson seems to
be a little ashamed that he is forced to use the term 'intuition.' [2] He
confesses that he hesitated for a long time to use the word, and apolo-
gizes for using it to express metaphysical activity, which is mainly the
inner cognition of spirit by spirit, and secondarily the cognition of
essence which exists in matter. We understand what Bergson means by
the word 'intuition': it is above all immediate consciousness. "Intuition
signifies first of all consciousness, immediate consciousness, a vision
which is hardly distinguished from the object seen, knowledge which
is contact and even coincidence." [3] But as far as it is immediate consciousness, it is not even distinguished from sensation or perception,
whereas metaphysics is by no means mere sense-perception. Bergson
is therefore forced to invent another kind of immediate consciousness.
"This experience, when it is concerned with a material object, will be
called vision, touch, or in general external perception, and when it
tends to spirit it will take the name of intuition." [4] This is a "super-
intellectual intuition." [5] As an example of intellectual intuition, we
have Aristotle's νοῦς, also immediate consciousness like sense-perception but yet concerned with intelligible objects. Does Bergson really
mean that his metaphysics is a system of intellectual νοῦς-like in-

[1] *Pensee*, p. 226.
[2] *Ibid.*, p. 243, n. 2 and p. 33.
[3] *Ibid.*, p. 35 f.
[4] *Ibid.*, p. 61.
[5] *Ibid.*, p. 34.

tuition? This is quite unplausible, for he is a firm anti-Aristotelian, though in fact his thought is not so divergent from Aristotle's as he imagined. Anyhow, the difference between Bergson's intuition and Aristotle's νοῦς is that intuition and its object, spirit, are in time [1] and movable, while νοῦς is concerned with eternal forms. According to Bergson, "the intuition of which he is talking is concerned first of all with inner duration. It seizes succession, which is not juxtaposition, a growth from inside, the uninterrupted prolongation of the past into the present which encroaches upon the future. This is the direct vision of spirit by spirit." [2] With regard to the ordinariness of this concept of time, we only suggest reference to Heidegger's criticism. [3] What is most important for the moment is to see how Bergson's spirit is situated in a lower order than is Aristotle's νοῦς. Instead of an eternal and universal principle, spirit is a formless entity changing and floating in time. It is a rather indefinite material principle which the Greeks called ὕλη. In other words, it is nothing but consciousness as a purely psychological phenomenon. Consequently, metaphysics which is yielded by such intuition is reduced to psychology, not the psychology as an objective positive science, but psychology in the vulgar sense of the word as a description of subjective consciousness. We wonder if it was really necessary to distinguish intuition from sensation for the sake of such a kind of metaphysics. We may distinguish spirit from matter by the differentiae of time and space. But to characterize spirit by its intelligibility, as distinct from our sensible consciousness, we cannot dispense with concepts. This way is, however, closed to Bergson by his own rejection of all intellectual elements from metaphysics.

Assuming that metaphysics is the intuition of spirit by spirit, where are its contents to come from? We might remind ourselves of Aristotle's idea νόησις νοήσεως. But Aristotle's metaphysics itself was not the result of νόησις νοήσεως. It was rather a system constituted from the cognition found in νοῦς and ἐπιστήμη, i.e. intellectual intuition and discursive reasoning. Thinking of thinking is, as Plotinus once pointed out, [4] not possible without presupposing the many. I suspect that Bergson's last chance to escape the barrenness into which his metaphysics might fall was to give metaphysics the extra, though subordinate, function of making insights into the spiritual elements in

---

[1] *Évolution*, p. 389.
[2] *Pensée*, p. 35.
[3] Heidegger, *Sein und Zeit*, p. 26.
[4] Plotinus, *Enn.* VI, 9, pp. 46 ff.

matter. Without this, his spirit would have had no alternative but to run counter to empiricism, just as the One of Plotinus did. Only it is doubtful whether this would have been effective enough to secure the safety of metaphysics. So as to keep its purity, metaphysics might rather have restricted itself to the region of pure spirit. When metaphysics calls to matter for help to escape barrenness, it can only keep its pride in its feeling or in other words in its method.

As expected, we find traces of Bergson's indecision about the distinction between metaphysics and science. In *Introduction to Metaphysics* (1903) [1] he says that not only our personality or spirit, but also external things, are in reality continuous. To these same objects, metaphysics and science apply different methods. The one uses intuition and penetrates them or sympathizes with their movement, the other uses understanding and analyses them or interprets their movements in terms of fixed symbols. According to this statement the object of both metaphysics and science seems to be matter as well as spirit, the only difference between metaphysics and science being found in their methods. And from this comes the difference in evaluation of the knowledge they yield. He says that metaphysics was true knowledge, while science was merely a convention. He could not have thought therefore that the object of science was reality. However, in the preface to the *Thought and what moves* (1922) [2] Bergson denies the distinction in value between metaphysics and science, and instead distinguishes them by their *objects* and methods. The opposition of intuitive and analytic methods is as before, but, in respect of their objects, metaphysics is considered to be concerned with spirit, while science treats matter. Both spirit and matter are parts of reality. Bergson re-emphasizes the idea that science is practical knowledge, but abandons the view that matter is mere appearance. He maintains that science reaches the essence of reality.

If matter and spirit are equally parts of reality and there is no difference in value or degree of existence between them, science cannot be relative knowledge nor can metaphysics be absolute. Bergson therefore is ambiguous when he says that science is concerned with a part of reality and may someday touch the bottom [3] or will approach the bottom indefinitely. [4] If this statement means that science is not actually touching reality when it investigates a thing, what does it

[1] Esp. p. 243, n. 2, 246, n. 1.
[2] *Pensée*, pp. 42, 52.
[3] *Ibid.*, p. 52.
[4] *Ibid.*

mean to touch reality potentially, apart from the suggestion that science is inferior to metaphysics? Further, if matter and spirit are not different aspects, but parts of reality, the distinction of science and metaphysics is similar to the distinction between natural science and mental science made by the Baden School to the effect that the one is the discovery of laws, the other the description of individual characters.

Bergson, to our surprise, restricts the object of positive science to inorganic bodies and delivers up the whole organic and spiritual world to metaphysics. [1] What is worse, he mentions, as a proof of its incapacity to know life, that intellect is merely a small part of evolutionary life. [2] I wonder if Bergson means by this that intuition or instinct is something more than a mere appearance of life, and that Bergson himself is something more than a living being? It is characteristic of realistic philosophy since Aristotle to determine the method of science by its object. If, however, matter and spirit are parts of reality, it is no less false to apprehend matter in motion than to apprehend spirit in a fixed state. Moreover, it is doubtful whether the opposition of spirit and matter is parallel to the opposition of movement and rest. Perhaps it is true that there is no rest in the spiritual world, as far as spirit is conceived as consciousness. But how can we deny movement in the material world except by the Eleatic paradox?

The fundamental presupposition of Bergson's philosophy is Cartesian dualism. Just as Descartes considered the attribute of mind to be consciousness and that of body extension, Bergson makes the attribute of spirit movement, that of matter rest. Just as, for Descartes, body and mind were both substances related with one another, for Bergson matter and spirit come into contact with each other. The relation between body and mind, which led Descartes into fatal difficulties, also leads Bergson into the same difficulties. Descartes' philosophy resulted in a queer theory of Occasionalism, whilst in Bergson matter and spirit are illicitly combined. Bergson would have liked to say that stationary matter was an illusion of moving spirit. But, being prohibited by twentieth century science, he fused matter and spirit in a less disquieting way. Claiming to use the Platonic concept of participation, he explains that matter participates [3] in spirit. He assures us that this participation will release matter from its state of

[1] *Évolution*, pp. 216, 213.
[2] *Ibid.*, II.
[3] *Pensée*, p. 37.

rest. Although by his fundamental presupposition matter must remain in a state of rest, Bergson argues as if it is true cognition to apprehend it in motion. This is a sophistry rather than a contradiction.

Bergson opposes metaphysics to science, but, being a modern philosopher, he cannot leave them in absolute separation. Moreover, he is French, and most French philosophers are very anxious to reconcile philosophy and science. He admits therefore that concepts are indispensable for intuition, [1] and says that all other sciences usually operate with concepts and metaphysics can be no exception.[2] This is just the same line of thought as Hegel's presupposition of the abstract analytical thinking of Understanding as the moment of speculation. Bergson's metaphysics is similar to Hegel's speculative philosophy in its transcendence of the Understanding. Bergson maintains that "metaphysics is properly itself only when it abandons concepts, or at least when it gets rid of rigid and ready-made concepts to create concepts quite different from those which we are accustomed to deal with." This demand for a concept beyond Understanding is also found in Hegel and Engels. But, being ignorant of dialectical method, there was no other way for Bergson but to go back to Sense instead of overcoming the limits of Understanding and reaching a higher stage of Reason. The required concept is "the representation which is elastic, moving, almost fluid, always ready to mould itself upon the fugitive forms of intuition," [3] the "representation which fits the object exclusively." [4]

To dissolve the conceptual system of metaphysics into such a chaos of fluctuating motions is to take the science out of metaphysics and make it into a form of art. Bergson coldly refused [5] to say anything about a person who commented that his intuition was merely instinct or feeling. But I wonder if he is not responsible for this comment. [6]

Unconceptualised metaphysics is not a real science. Intuition may be called a kind of cognition, but not every cognition is a science. In Bergson, positive science and metaphysics are not species of any genus. For he restricts science mainly to positive science. The definition of metaphysics is also negative and incomplete. He talks only of its distinction from science. Take away the science, and reality reveals itself,

---

[1] *Ibid.*, pp. 211. 39.
[2] *Ibid.*
[3] *Ibid.*, p. 213.
[4] *Ibid.*, p. 223.
[5] *Ibid.*, p. 107.
[6] Cf. *Évolution*, pp. 162, 165, 173, 191, 192 f., 197, 289.

and there is metaphysics! "We attribute to the state of mind fixedness, discontinuity, and generality of words. We must take this envelope and tear it open. The spatiality and what is spatial in this sense are here the real causes of the relativity of our knowledge. Taking off this interposed veil, we return to the immediate and touch an absolute."[1] As if not only the absolute being but also its knowledge were ready-made by God, and science was nothing but an obstacle. Is metaphysics really the Grace of God instead of the Fruit of Wisdom?

Bergson protests against the criticism that his theory of knowledge is too optimistic. He maintains that intuition is not relaxation, but reflexion and strain. [2] However, even restricting it to the cognition of our own spirit or of another person's, how is it possible to prove that the intuition which we believe ourselves to have seized by merely taking away the symbols is really philosophical knowledge? Philosophical cognition is said to be the intuition which enters into the thing and unites with it. But what actual significance is there in the effort which is required for philosophy apart from the refusal to admit scientific knowledge? I could not repress my suspicions, if it were not that they were the apology of an idle Reason.

In short, from its presuppositions Bergson's theory of knowledge should have led to an absolute denial of science and to mysticism. Whereas on the contrary he assumes that science and philosophy will go forward helping each other. This is the self-protection of a mystic born in the age of positivism. But how can he possibly get cooperation between quite heterogeneous cognitions? His explanation is very obscure and unsatisfactory – "Just because they are on the same level, they have points in common and can verify these points with each other ... The results obtained from each side should join up, since matter joins up with spirit. If the fit is not perfect, it will be because there is something to be redressed in our science or in our metaphysics, or in both. The metaphysics will thus exercise, through its periphery, a salutary influence on the science. The science inversely will communicate to the metaphysics the habits of precision which will spread from the periphery of metaphysics to its centre." [3] Such an easy pro-

---

[1] *Pensée*, p. 28. Cf. *Évolution*, p. 217.

[2] *Pensée*, p. 109 f.

[3] *Pensée*, p. 53 f. 31 f. "For inexactitude usually means the inclusion of a thing in too wide a genus. On the other hand, things and genus correspond to pre-existing words. But if one begins by discarding the ready-made concepts, if one gives oneself to a direct and real vision, if one then subdivides this reality, taking into account its articulations, the new concepts which one forms will be this time tailored to the exact measurements of the object. The inexactitude only arises through extending these concepts to other objects which they

mise can by no means set us at ease. Were not matter and spirit two heterogeneous areas of reality, to be recognised by the contrary methods of analysis and sympathy? What a curious mongrel will result from the mixture of these quite heterogeneous strains when metaphysics exercises some useful influence upon science (though what such influence could be, I don't know), science in return gives exactness to metaphysics, and this strange influence and habit spreads from the periphery to the centre. We cannot now pass over the fact that Bergson was the President of the Society of Psychical Research. If the useful influence of metaphysics is not intuition, and the exactness of science not analysis, then what in the world are they? If they *are* so, then what is the difference between Bergson's position and the mistaken science and metaphysics of the past, which confused the methods of investigating matter and spirit? As is usual with a dualist, Bergson is keen to distinguish intelligence and intuition, practice and contemplation, science and metaphysics, but he stumbles and stammers when he begins to interrelate them.

It was Bergson's fervent desire, just as it was Kant's, to save metaphysics from the despotism of science. But the divorce was not an easy task, as had been at first imagined. Metaphysics was like a gallant who, being weary of a sterling housewife "Understanding," yet without the brilliant wit necessary to become intimate with a lady "Reason," has found comfort in a street girl "Intuition," but, to avoid scandal, has begged forgiveness from the wife he has betrayed.

2. HEIDEGGER

Heidegger's philosophical interest has been confined to metaphysics. He declares proudly that metaphysics is the destiny of Europe and that the German nation as the inheritor of the Greek metaphysical tradition is especially entrusted with a world-historical mission. [1] Such a boastful remark seems somewhat ridiculous now after the downfall of Nazism, in defence of which it was made. At least it cannot give a pleasant impression except to a German, and one might retort that, if metaphysics is the speciality of the German nation, such metaphysics

---

will embrace equally in their generality. But they must be studied in themselves outside these concepts, if one wants to know them in turn." If this is the real meaning of exactitude, metaphysics does not need to borrow it from science. For in this sense metaphysics is originally exact. We must rather say that metaphysics has its exactitude *sui generis*. To say like Bergson that metaphysics borrows its exactitude from science is just *qui s'excuse, s'accuse*.

[1] Heidegger, *Einführung in die Metaphysik*, pp. 28 ff.

cannot belong to universal culture. At any rate, according to Heidegger
Sein has been the main problem of philosophy since the Greeks, but
already in antiquity a fundamental mistake was made with regard to
this problem. For the Greeks regarded 'to be' as the most general and
therefore the emptiest concept, and thought that, being self-evident,
it did not need to be defined. Heidegger, however, considers that 'to be'
is neither a general concept nor self-evident, though it cannot be
defined. Metaphysics or ontology in a wider sense inquired into being
instead of into 'to be.' Metaphysics always confused 'to be' with being,
and, though it maintained that it dealt with 'to be,' really it only
treated of being. [1] Plato, Aristotle and Kant indeed distinguished ontology from the special sciences. According to them, ontology inquires
into the grounds of the possibility of being. But, insofar as these ontologies neglected to expound the meaning of 'to be,' they were defective. [2]

That metaphysics inquired into being instead of into 'to be' is a
favourite idea of Heidegger's. He even repeats it in his later works
when his conception of metaphysics has changed. What is it then to
inquire into 'to be' *qua* 'to be?' Seeing that Aristotle and Kant, who
distinguished metaphysics from the special sciences, the first as a
science which inquired into being in general, and the second as a science
which asked the conditions of the possibility of being, both these
philosophers are rejected as having dealt only with being instead of
'to be,' we feel the extraordinary character of the problem of inquiring
into the 'to be.' Indeed, this kind of mystification seems to be the secret
of Heidegger's charm. But is it true that every metaphysical theory
in the past asked what being is and neglected the question of what
'to be' is? Does Heidegger really mean to say that Plato's Ideas were
mere being and not the principle which made both being and the
knowledge of being possible? Suppose that this were so. But what
about Aristotle's metaphysics? Did Aristotle not inquire into the
problem of 'to be' in being, when he dealt with the various meanings
of 'being?' Further, did not Berkeley both raise and offer a solution
to the problem of 'to be' when he said '*esse est percipi?*' Why must
Kant not be held to have inquired into 'to be' *qua* 'to be,' when he
maintained that being was an absolute 'positing?' Finally, in what
sense does Heidegger himself inquire into 'to be' *qua* 'to be,' an inquiry
which, according to him, all past metaphysics has neglected?

[1] I translated *Seiendes* by 'being,' and *Sein* by 'to be,' but the former may be rendered in
'what exists,' the latter in 'being.'
[2] *Sein und Zeit*, p. 2.

We might ask whether an inquiry into 'to be' *qua* 'to be' should take the form of the question he raises in his books, *Was ist Metaphysik?* and *Einführung in die Metaphysik*, namely "Why does being exist and not nothingness?"[1] But although this question is called by Heidegger the most extensive, the most profound, and the most fundamental of all questions, [2] he himself admits it to be a question of "metaphysics." Indeed, Christian theology, though in the semi-mythological form of a theory of creation, raised the question, "Why does being exist and not nothingness?," and answered that it was because God wanted and created being by means of his will. Hegel, in his *Science of Logic*, showed us the dialectic of being and nothingness before entering into the theory of existence (*Dasein*). It was surely a metaphysical speculation of high order that sought the secret of 'to be' behind being. As in all these historical examples of metaphysical speculation Heidegger accuses the metaphysicians of neglecting the problem of what 'to be' is, we must expect that Heidegger's question is somewhat different from the metaphysical question which he formulates in the words, "Why does being exist and not nothingness?" or "Why is there something and not nothing?"

However, without precisely explaining either the meaning of the question, what 'to be' *qua* 'to be' is, nor how such a question should be answered, Heidegger inquires into the conditions of an inquiry into 'to be' itself. According to him, it must be explained from the analysis of a certain particular being [3] and not of any particular being one likes. That particular being is the being, who asks this question, viz., *Dasein*.

We should never finish if we worried about Heidegger's peculiar terminology. But the word *Dasein* contains an extremely important idea, in which the secret of his whole philosophy is concealed, and we might say that Heidegger spent his whole life interpreting this single word. Unfortunately we cannot expect to succeed, however scrupulously we may try to explain his concept with the usual terminology of traditional philosophy. Every attempt of this kind necessarily appears superficial and misleading. The more clear and distinct the explanation, the more unfavourable is the interpreter's situation. For what this dark philosopher of the Black Forest aims at with his curious terminology is not illumination as he claims, but really mystification. Following and imitating his great predecessor of Ephesus, he purposely conceals his truth from the eyes of ordinary people.

[1] *Was ist Metaphysik?*, p. 38; *Einführung*, pp. 1 ff.
[2] *Einführung*, pp. 2 ff.
[3] *Sein und Zeit*, p. 7.

Needless to say, *Dasein* must not be understood in its usual sense of existence in time and space. Not that there is something accidentally there, but the 'there' (*da*) which is an element of that being (*Dasein*) forms the 'to be' of that being itself. Of course such an explanation is not easily understood by an ordinary man. But when the interpreter takes a step forward, he must be prepared to be accused of shallowness. The fear of this accusation often drives a diffident student to become a disciple busying himself with mimicry. If we risk this accusation and hazard the suggestion that *Dasein* is after all a kind of consciousness, [1] only not consciousness as a particular phenomenon, but an omnipotent consciousness which is the condition of every appearance of being, Heidegger's philosophy simply becomes a modification of transcendental idealism (we must apologise if this is too shallow a distortion). Let us then attend to the ingenious expression of this deep philosopher. *Dasein* is superior to other beings insofar as it understands its own existence. The *ontic* superiority of *Dasein* is due to its ontological character. Of course, in this immediate stage of understanding the 'to be,' we have not yet ontology as a theory. *Dasein* is only ontological insofar as it exists understanding that it exists. The 'to be' of *Dasein* is existence, its understanding is called *existentiell*. The structure of existence is existentiality, its analysis is by means of *existential* understanding – this must be distinguished from mere *existentiell* understanding. The possibility and necessity of an existential analysis of *Dasein* is shown beforehand in the structure of the 'to be' of Dasein. [2] Let us dismiss for the present the introduction of the Scholastic analysis, which Heidegger learned from his teacher Husserl. What is more important for us is that science is a mode of *Dasein*, and that, since *Dasein* is in the world, the understanding of the 'to be' which belongs to *Dasein* involves the understanding of the 'to be' of both the world and beings in the world. [3] Thus the science of beings other than *Dasein* is based upon the structure of *Dasein*. Heidegger calls this basic theory fundamental ontology, and says that it grows from the existential analysis of *Dasein*. [4]

To resume our argument, Heidegger says that every metaphysical theory has inquired into being *qua* being and neglected the inquiry into 'to be' *qua* 'to be.' However, instead of giving an explicit expla-

[1] I do not forget Heidegger's protest against such an interpretation. Cf. *Was ist Metaphysik?*, p. 15.
[2] *Sein und Zeit*, p. 12 f.
[3] *Ibid.*, p. 13.
[4] *Ibid.*

nation of what it means to inquire into 'to be,' he only maintains that his fundamental ontology is the foundation of all ontologies. Hence we can infer that at least the existential analysis of *Dasein* is a part of the ontology he offers.

At first Heidegger aimed at establishing a whole system of ontology upon this foundation. But he could not complete the system. This is just like the case of Kant. Seen from the point of view of his actual achievement Heidegger's ontology appears as the theory of human existence which he called *Dasein*. Even if we judge his philosophy from the point of view of what he hoped to achieve, ontology as the science of 'to be' must be built upon the ontology of human being. This differs from past ontology in that it is either the analysis of *Dasein* instead of the science of being in general, or at least it is founded upon such an ontology. It is a subjective ontology viewed from the special point of view of *Dasein*. It is opposed for example to N. Hartmann's objective ontology, in a manner similar to the opposition between Kant and Wolff.

According to Heidegger, *Dasein* is qualified to be the foundation of the whole of ontology through its superiority in the following three respects. [1]

1. *ontic* superiority of existence,
2. ontological superiority,
3. superiority in being the foundation of other ontological theories.

This is just the same line of thinking as Aristotle's when he regarded metaphysics on the one hand as the science which inquires into being *qua* being universally, and, on the other hand, made it the science of the first substance, pure form, or God, and identified it with theology. Now what difference is there between the superiority of *Dasein* to other modes of being, and the superiority of God to other substances? Heidegger explains the superiority of *Dasein* as consisting in its being the ontic, ontological, and ontic-ontological condition of other beings. But is not this the same as the relation of God to other substances, but for the peculiarity of Heidegger's terminology? For thinking about thinking is the essential activity of God, and God is just the being as to whom the 'to be' of his being is the problem. Further, His self-contemplation moves other things by being itself the object of love; he is the archetype of the thinking activities of every other spiritual being. Taking these similarities into account, we may duly call Aristotle's theology a fundamental ontology in Heidegger's sense. A genuine

[1] *Ibid.*

materialist might say that God is a mere imagined idea; that it is only a reflection of human existence; that, however rich the concept might be, its instantiation cannot be guaranteed at all. Although Heidegger's *Dasein* is an individual, it must not be confused with the individual animal of Feuerbach's or Engel's conception. If an existentialist denies the existence of God, he *ipso facto* annihilates his own *Dasein*. The situation is the same even if one says that God is an element of *Dasein* as *In-der-Welt-sein*. The reason why the existential analysis of *Dasein* is the fundamental ontology is this. Since *Dasein* is *In-der-Welt-sein*, the understanding of the 'to be' by *Dasein* includes the understanding both of the 'to be' of the world and of the being in the world. But this proof is unsatisfactory, for it is quite possible that *Dasein* comprehends only one aspect of the world. To exclude this possibility, one must prove that the world is nothing more than a mere moment of *Dasein*, nothing more than our representation. *Dasein* can be *In-der-Welt-sein* as far as *Welt* is outside *Dasein*, otherwise we should call the *Welt In-dem-Ich-sein* rather than calling *Dasein In-der-Welt-sein*. In saying this, I do not ignore Heidegger's assertion that the 'in' in *in-sein* is not a spatial relation, but is rather a relation of interest. In whatever sense the *in* may be taken, the transcendence of the world cannot be denigrated. The ontology built upon the analysis of *Dasein* gives us only a subjective view of the world, as compared to science which gives us objective knowledge. Thus, Heidegger's ontology is subjective knowledge, just like Bergson's metaphysics. Like Bergson, Heidegger explains the structure of *Dasein* through the conception of time. But, unlike Bergson, he interprets the 'to be' in terms of temporality, [1] which he distinguishes from the traditional notion of time, the one being purely subjective, the other more or less objective – though Heidegger would not like such a shallow explanation. Heidegger himself characterizes temporality as historical. The modes of *Dasein* are historical. This characteristic of *Dasein* is made possible by temporality. In the traditional way of thinking, the historical character of *Dasein* was concealed. In the ordinary way of being, *Dasein* 'has fallen into' the world and tradition. The ontology of the past interpreted *Dasein* from the world; it 'has fallen into' tradition and could not be conscious of the historical character of *Dasein*. To get rid of this rigidity and concealment Heidegger demands the rejection of ancient ontology. [2]

According to Heidegger, Kant noticed that time was the foundation

[1] *Ibid.*, p. 18.
[2] *Ibid.*, p. 22.

of being, but could not explain the relation between time and *cogito* because he neglected the problems of 'to be.' Also, he did not have an ontology of *Dasein*, and understood the concept of time in the traditional and ordinary way. Descartes also assumed the *sum* to be self-evident and did not ask its meaning. Following mediaeval ontology he set up *res cogitans* as *res creata*. To assess the result brought about by Descartes' following the mediaeval ontology, we must explain the limits and meanings of ancient ontology.

In ancient philosophy, being was regarded as existing in the world or in nature and its 'to be' was interpreted through the conception of time. For example, παρουσία or οὐσία means 'to be present' (*Anwesenheit*). Such being is understood from a certain mode of time, i.e. from the present. But, in the Greek interpretation of being, the fundamental ontological function of time was not known, and time was treated as a kind of being. This interpretation of time determined all later theories, and Kant and Bergson were no exceptions. To make the problem of 'to be' more concrete, Heidegger needs to get outside this tradition. [1] Let us dismiss for the moment the question of the validity of Heidegger's criticism of the concept of time used by Aristotle and Kant. I can at least understand what Heidegger intends. Using our superficial terms, he wants to establish a radically subjective notion of time through which he can interpret the world. This is a subjective deviation from Husserl's phenomenology.

Heidegger actually adopted phenomenology [2] as the method of his ontology. According to him, the phenomenon disclosed by phenomenology is the 'to be' of being. The content of phenomenology is ontology. The fundamental ontology is the ontology of *Dasein*, its method being *hermeneutics*. Hermeneutics is employed secondarily as the method of other ontologies and of the historical sciences. The 'to be' of being is not a genus, but a *transcendentale*, its cognition being transcendental. The phenomenological truth or the disclosure of 'to be' is a transcendental truth. Ontology and phenomenology are not two branches of philosophy. From the point of view of the object, philosophy is ontology, from that of its method, it is phenomenology. Philosophy is the universal phenomenological ontology which starts from the hermeneutics of *Dasein*. [3] This is a summary of the arguments on the design of his new ontology set out in his main work *Sein und Zeit* in 1927.

[1] *Ibid.*, pp. 24 ff.
[2] *Ibid.*, pp. 27 ff.
[3] *Ibid.*, p. 38.

Many problems are suggested. We may find very interesting subjects of inquiry in the relations between the phenomenologies of Heidegger, Husserl, and Hegel; also between Heidegger's transcendentalism and Kant's transcendental philosophy. These problems however must be put aside lest we should make our argument too complex. We would content ourselves with the confirmation that, in respect of method, Heidegger's new ontology was nothing more than a phenomenology.

It is a somewhat disappointing discovery that the 'to be' of being is nothing but the phenomenon which is to be explained by phenomenology. 'Being' of course appears. But if the 'to be' of being is dissolved into phenomena, where is the *raison d'être* of metaphysics or ontology? It is true that Husserl tried to expand the concept of 'phenomenon' as far as possible. Nevertheless, if we remove finitude from the definition of 'phenomenon,' what is left? And if we remove infinity from being, in virtue of what does it deserve the name of being? For phenomenology to coincide with ontology, the screen on which the 'to be' of being is projected must be the infinite reason of God. Whereas Heidegger's screen is a small individual, whether or not we choose to dignify it with the name of *Dasein*. This subjective tendency of Heidegger's in his early work *Sein und Zeit* is, however, modified in his later works with a more objective interpretation. But before examining this modification we must investigate another important work of his early period, *Kant und das Problem der Metaphysik*.

In this work, which consists of lectures delivered in 1925 and 1926, and then published in 1929, Heidegger stands, in the main, on the same ground as he held in *Sein und Zeit*. There is a slight difference, in that in the previous work he talked mainly of the relations between ontology and phenomenology, but seldom used the term 'metaphysics.' This is because in the previous work he meant by 'ontology' not a branch of traditional metaphysics, but a new science which studied in a general way the 'to be' of being, whereas now he treats ontology as falling within the framework of traditional metaphysics, and subject to the Wolff-Baumgarten definition of *metaphysica generalis*. [1] He defines fundamental ontology as the metaphysics of human being (*Dasein*) which makes metaphysics (i.e. *specialis*) possible. From the fact that Kant used the term 'transcendental philosophy' synonymously with 'ontology,' Heidegger concludes that Kant's *Critique of Pure Reason* was an ontology and not a theory of knowledge, and that this ontology was the foundation of metaphysics, which, starting from

[1] *Kant und das Problem der Metaphysik*, p. 15.

metaphysica generalis, aimed at the determination of *metaphysica specialis*. [1] This is also M. Wundt's opinion. I agree with them in their judgement that Kant's Critique was the foundation of a new metaphysics, though we must notice that Kant did not call his Critique 'transcendental philosophy' in the sense of 'the science of *transcendentalia*.'

Now, according to Heidegger, Kant's foundation of metaphysics leads to transcendental imagination, the common root of Sense and Understanding. This root is planted in the original temporality. Therefore the question of the 'to be,' the fundamental question of the foundation of metaphysics, is the problem of *Sein und Zeit*. This title contains the guiding idea for an interpretation of the *Critique of Pure Reason* as the foundation of metaphysics. The idea proved by this interpretation gives us the form of the problem of fundamental ontology. We must not understand this idea as setting itself up as 'new' and opposing itself to what is old. It is rather the expression of the effort to penetrate the essence of the foundation of metaphysics in its original form, through refounding it. [2]

Heidegger distinguishes the result (*Resultat*) and effect (*Ergebnis*) of Kant's foundation of metaphysics. The result is the admission of transcendental imagination and temporality as the foundation of transcendence. Its effect is the demonstration of human subjectivity. According to Kant's *Grundlegung*, the foundation of metaphysics is the inquiry into man, i.e. anthropology. [3] Kant's anthropology, however, could not succeed as it was empirical. What is needed is philosophical anthropology. Kant himself admitted that in founding metaphysics he aimed at forging links between anthropology and metaphysics. The purpose of this work is to give foundations to 'metaphysics in its ultimate end,' viz., *metaphysica specialis*, to which belong three disciplines: cosmology, psychology, and theology. The Critique of Pure Reason must include these disciplines in its intrinsic essence, if man really takes metaphysics to be his natural disposition. The fundamental essence of human reason manifests itself in its interests, with which, insofar as it is human reason, it is constantly preoccupied. These are: (1) What can I know? (2) What should I do? (3) What may I hope? Corresponding to these three problems there are three branches of *metaphysica specialis:* Cosmology, Psychology, and The-

---

[1] *Ibid.*, p. 25.
[2] *Ibid.*, p. 183.
[3] *Ibid.*, p. 186.

ology. These problems and branches of metaphysics are reduced to the problem "What is man?" and to Anthropology respectively. Consequently, a repetition of Kant's foundation of metaphysics is a formation of a system of philosophical anthropology. According to Heidegger, 'anthropology' at the present time must not signify a branch of science, but must signify an attitude of man towards himself and towards being as a whole. It does not merely seek truths about man, but rather, it decides what is truth in general. Philosophical anthropology therefore means philosophy in general. [1]

Now the term 'philosophical anthropology' was first employed by M. Scheler. But in Heidegger's view Scheler did not sufficiently explain the essence of this science. Not every anthropology is the foundation of metaphysics. An anthropology may sometimes be unconscious of its function as the foundation of metaphysics. So, before starting on the question 'What is man?,' we must ask why, in the foundation of metaphysics in general, only man is to be investigated. In other words, we must ask why the three problems of *metaphysica specialis* should be reduced to the fourth problem. Now, the three problems concern possibility, obligation, and the hope of man; all of these being found only in finite being. They are bound up with the finitude of human reason. Consequently the foundation of metaphysics attempts to answer the question of the finitude of man. [2]

Kant's foundation of metaphysics began by justifying the basis of metaphysics proper (*metaphysica specialis*), i.e. by justifying *metaphysica generalis*. What was in antiquity, especially in Aristotle, the problem of first philosophy, of philosophical thought in the authentic sense, received the fixed form of a discipline; it was fixed as *metaphysica generalis* and called ontology. In Aristotle, it was not obvious what connection the question of ὄν ᾗ ὄν, being *qua* being, had with the question of being as a whole (θεῖον). The term 'metaphysics' represents a dubious concept. [3] Not only is the question of the two fundamental dimensions of the problem of being highly controversial, but also the question of their possible unity. Therefore if the question of man's finitude has to be decided by a process of refounding metaphysics, it must be released from the fixed system of school metaphysics. This implies that one cannot accept the Aristotelian way of posing the problem as definitive. From the question of 'What is being?' we cannot

---

[1] *Ibid.*, p. 187 f.
[2] *Ibid.*, p. 195.
[3] *Ibid.*, p. 199.

derive the question of man's finitude. So, in repeating Kant's foundation work, we must explain the essential reference between the 'to be' and the finitude of man. [1]

It was Aristotle who first distinguished two dimensions in the general problem of being by Natural Philosophers. In this way he set up, though vaguely, an order of precedence among the two questions. Namely, first the problem of 'What is being?'; second the problem of being as a whole. But the question what being is is too vague. It is really the question what determines being *qua* being, i.e. the 'to be' of being. Therefore before the question of what is being *qua* being, we must ask what the 'to be' itself is. [2]

The *Was-sein* of being is called *essentia, possibilitas,* ἰδέα etc., and *Daß-Sein* is called *existentia*. The relation between *essentia* and *existentia* presupposes an answer to the question what the 'to be' is? And, besides, the 'to be' also means 'truth.' To solve these problems of the 'to be,' we must go back from the question what the 'to be' is to the question how the 'to be' is to be explained. [3] It is difficult to see that the problem of the 'to be' has any essential connection with the finitude of man. Philosophical thinking faces the problem of being insofar as this problem belongs to the essence of philosophy. And philosophy is one of man's possibilities. The problem of the 'to be' is not a contrived question; it springs from the preconceptual understanding [4] of the 'to be' which we have insofar as we are men. Consequently, taken more profoundly, the problem of the foundation leads to an exhibition of the inner possibility of interpreting the 'to be.' Though it is obvious that we stand in various relations to other beings, the 'to be' of beings remains obscure. Hegel said that pure 'to be' is nothing, but this is not true, for we are constantly understanding the 'to be' of beings. This ordinary understanding, however, is not cognition (*Erkenntnis*), but mere acquaintance (*Bekenntnis*). Man is a specially qualified being, in whom both he himself and other beings will be revealed. This special state is called *Existenz*. Human being presupposes and depends upon other beings. All beings are revealed to this finite being. The understanding of being is essential to finite being; there is no need to ask about the relationship between human finitude and the understanding of being. This relationship is essential and necessary. Now man is what he is in virtue of being *Dasein*.

[1] *Ibid.,* p. 200.
[2] *Ibid.,* p. 201.
[3] *Ibid.,* p. 202 f.
[4] *Ibid.,* p. 204.

The foundation of metaphysics is the question of the *Dasein* of man ;
it is *per se* metaphysics. Kant was conscious of this; so his Critique is a
metaphysics of metaphysics rather than a theory of knowledge. [1]

The metaphysics of *Dasein* as the foundation of metaphysics is not
a metaphysics about *Dasein*. It is a metaphysics which necessarily
comes into existence as a mode of *Dasein*. [2] *Dasein's* apprehension of
the 'to be' reveals itself in ontology. The ontology which gives the
foundation to metaphysics is fundamental ontology. It makes explicit
what we are acquainted with but do not yet recognize. It brings to
light the 'to be' from the recesses of memory. The refounding of metaphysics results in the problem of explaining the temporality which
is the transcendental constitution of *Dasein*, and the problem of interpreting the essence of conscience, obligation, and death in order to
disclose man's finitude. Metaphysics is not created as a dogma, but
is an event in *Dasein*. [3] As an interpretation of Kant, Heidegger's
book is an immature and defective work of narrow vision. Nevertheless
it helps us to understand Heidegger's ontology in relation to the history of philosophy. Though we agree with Heidegger in regarding
Kant's Critique as the foundation of metaphysics, we can by no means
accept his undue emphasis on transcendental imagination and time.
But the theory that the foundation of metaphysics leads on to anthropology is more plausible. Heidegger's interpretation of Kant's Critique
as resulting in the disclosure of human subjectivity suggests inter-
estingly the connection between his ontology and Kant's transcendental philosophy. But his interpretation of Aristotle's metaphysics is far
from being satisfactory. To interpret θεῖον as being as a whole is inexact
and even misleading. θεῖον must be literally translated as 'divine.' [4]
The science of divine being is theology, whereas the science of being
as a whole is ontology. If θεῖον were interpreted as 'being as a whole,'
there would be no opposition at all between ontology and theology, for
there is no real opposition between the question of being *qua* being and
the question of being as a whole. Further, as we have already explained,
Aristotle's view of the relation between these two different questions

[1] *Ibid.*, p. 207 f.
[2] *Ibid.*, p. 208.
[3] *Ibid.*, p. 218.
[4] In *Kant*, etc., Heidegger translated θεῖον to "das Seiende im Ganzen" through connecting
"das Seiende als Seiende" (ὄν ᾗ ὄν)" with "der vorzüglichste Bezirk des Seienden (τιμιώτατον
γένος)" using "das Seiende im Ganzen (καθόλου)" as the middle term. But it is unreasonable
to apply "das Seiende im Ganzen" which he used for translating καθόλου here to θεῖον.
Besides, καθόλου is "das Allgemeine," not "das Seiende im Ganzen." In *Was ist Metaphysik?*
p. 18, Heidegger counts both ὄν καθόλου, κοινόν and ὄν καθόλου, ἀκρότατον θεῖον as two
modes of representation of the beingness of the being.

is similar to Heidegger's view of the relation between fundamental and special ontologies. Heidegger's criticism of Aristotle for neglecting the solution is therefore unjustified. But the minute examination of Heidegger's interpretation of historical theories is not our present concern.

Now, according to Heidegger, Kant's Critique of Pure Reason was intended to be the foundation of metaphysics, and was itself an ontology. In refounding metaphysics, Heidegger aims at establishing fundamental ontology – a strange notion indeed, because ontology is essentially fundamental metaphysics and a special ontology is a *contradictio in adjecto*. Heidegger's terminology presupposes the identification of ontology with metaphysics, which is in fact a tendency of recent academic philosophy. Heidegger did not however go into the relationship between ontology and fundamental ontology. He describes his fundamental ontology as the metaphysics of *Dasein*. Here we can see a trace of regression from the peculiar concept of ontology in *Sein und Zeit* to the traditional concept of metaphysics. Heidegger actually holds to his previous criticism of traditional metaphysics, viz. that it has always been a science of being and has ignored the problem of the 'to be.' And for this reason he asks us to reject traditional metaphysics. But he no longer demands that we should abandon the concept of metaphysics. Just as with Kant and Hegel, Heidegger's concept of metaphysics is ambiguous between metaphysical theories in the past and metaphysics as a branch of philosophy. His new theory of the 'to be' seems to be comprehended in the latter sense of metaphysics. The concept of metaphysics is the main subject of *Was ist Metaphysik?*, which consists in a lecture delivered in 1929, with a supplement added in 1934, and an introduction added in 1951. Another lecture given in 1935 was published with no important modification in 1953, under the title of *Einführung in die Metaphysik. Vom Wesen der Wahrheit* appeared in 1943, *Über Humanismus* – a letter to Jean Beaufret – in 1946. These were followed by many works, most of which are fragmentary or ephemeral writings. This fragmentary character of his later works, together with the tendency towards mystification, suggests a decline in Heidegger's speculative thinking. In these later works Heidegger is busy interpreting his main work, but, as is usually the case, repeated interpretations are apt to modify the original thought. We shall examine these modifications later.

In *Was ist Metaphysik?* Heidegger distinguishes metaphysics from science in that the latter is concerned with being and neglects nothingness, while the former inquires into nothingness. Metaphysics may in this way transcend being and inquires into the 'to be' of being. [1] This is the same thought, expressed in a slightly modified way, as he previously put in words such as that the 'to be' is revealed through the finitude of *Dasein,* or that the analysis of *Dasein* is the first step of fundamental ontology. Interesting as it is, this is a fine example of dialectic. For the disclosure of the 'to be' which transcends being is attained through the medium of nothingness. In other words, metaphysics as the science of being must, at the same time, be the science of nothingness. Now metaphysics is understood as the science of the 'to be' instead of the science of being as it was characterised in *Sein und Zeit.* It is either a remarkable change in Heidegger's terminology, or a careless confusion. "Metaphysics is an inquiry over and above being, with a view to winning it back again as such and as a whole for our understanding. In our quest for nothingness there is a similar transcendence from being, conceived as being as a whole. It therefore turns out to be a metaphysical question."[2] Thus the questions about nothingness are shown to be metaphysical. " 'To be' and nothingness hang together but not because the two things – from the point of view of the Hegelian concept of thought – are one in their indefiniteness and immediateness, but because 'to be' itself is finite in essence and is only revealed in the transcendence of *Dasein* as projected into nothingness. If indeed the question of the 'to be' as such is the all-embracing question of metaphysics, then the question of nothingness proves to be such as to span the whole metaphysical field."[3] "Only in the nothingness of *Dasein* can being as a whole – and this in accordance with its peculiar possibilities, i.e. in a finite manner – come to itself."[4] "But now in this question of nothingness, it becomes evident that scientific *Dasein* is only possible when projected into nothingness at the outset. It understands itself in that in which it stands only when it does not abandon nothingness. The alleged sobriety and superiority of science become ridiculous if it fails to take nothingness seriously. Only because nothingness is obvious can science turn being into an object of investigation. Only when science proceeds from metaphysics can it obtain its essential problem ever afresh ..."[5] "The inquiry into nothingness puts us, the inquirers, ourselves in question. It is

[1] *Was ist Metaphysik?,* p. 36.
[2] *Ibid.*
[3] *Ibid.*
[4] *Ibid.*
[5] *Ibid.,* p. 37.

a metaphysical one." [1] Man's *Dasein* can only relate to being by projecting into nothingness. Transcendence of being is of the essence of *Dasein*. But this transcendency is metaphysics itself. That is why metaphysics belongs to the nature of man ... Metaphysics is the ground-phenomenon of *Dasein*. It is *Dasein* itself ... Hence scientific strictness can not hope to equal the seriousness of metaphysics. Philosophy can never be measured with the yard-stick of the idea of science." [2]

In this way, metaphysics becomes more clearly the science of 'to be' and is opposed to science which is concerned with being. We no longer find the concept of ontology or fundamental ontology. This corresponds to the following statement in *Einführung in die Metaphysik:* "Since the term 'ontology' is used in academic philosophy to mean a branch of philosophy, and academic philosophers refuse to attempt any solution to the problem of the 'to be,' it might be better to refrain from using the term 'ontology.'" [3] Similarly in the preface [4] to *Was ist Metaphysik?* supplemented in 1951, Heidegger says that he found the term 'fundamental ontology' which he used in *Sein und Zeit* to be unsuitable because it suggested that fundamental ontology was itself a kind of ontology. He considers that the thinking which aims at grasping the truth of the 'to be' regresses to the basis of metaphysics so that it is different from any area of ontology. But in this argument we cannot avoid the same difficulty, even if we use an expression such as 'metaphysics of metaphysics' or 'metaphysics of *Dasein*.' For, just as fundamental ontology appeared to be a kind of ontology, though it was not really so, metaphysics of metaphysics or metaphysics of *Dasein* appeared to be a mere species or branch of metaphysics. And provided that metaphysics is the science which deals with being instead of the 'to be,' the metaphysics of *Dasein* cannot avoid the appearance of being also the science of some special kind of being. When Heidegger at first employed in *Sein und Zeit* the concept of ontology, he meant to distinguish ontology as the science of the 'to be' from metaphysics as the science of being. But now it seems on the contrary as if ontology is the science of being whilst metaphysics is the science of the 'to be.' At the same time, in the preface [5] of *Was ist Meta-*

---

[1] *Ibid.*
[2] *Ibid.*
[3] *Einführung*, p. 31. Cf. *Humanismus*, p. 110.
[4] *Was ist Metaphysik?*, p. 19.
[5] *Ibid.*, p. 11.

physik?, and in *Einführung in die Metaphysik* [1] etc., Heidegger repeats, perhaps unconscious of his inconsistency, that metaphysics
neglected to inquire into the 'to be' and only concerned itself with
being. Thus the thinking which reveals the 'to be' cannot be suitably
called either ontology or fundamental ontology, or metaphysics of
metaphysics or metaphysics of *Dasein*. It is most ironical that metaphysics or ontology ends up as the *"Ausdruck der Verlegenheit"* [2] for
Heidegger himself rather than for Aristotle.

"The question, 'What is metaphysics?' asks a question that goes
beyond metaphysics. It arises from a way of thinking which has already entered into the overcoming of metaphysics." [3] "... then we
must necessarily ask what metaphysics is on its own ground. Such a
question must think metaphysically and, at the same time, think
in terms of the ground of metaphysics, i.e. no longer metaphysically. All such questions must remain equivocal in an essential
sense." [4] This is not, however, peculiar to Heidegger's thinking, but
may be applied both to Kant's transcendental philosophy and to
Hegel's logic. They both originate in metaphysics, examine it, return
to it, and maintain it at a higher level. This is the essential difference
between these philosophies and the ordinary theories of knowledge in
academic philosophy, which merely oppose themselves to metaphysics.
But Heidegger's embarrassment seems to be on the point whether to
call the thinking beyond metaphysics metaphysics or to call it by some
other name. In the preface [5] to *Was ist Metaphysik?*, Heidegger,
quoting Descartes, compares metaphysics to the root, and the truth of
the 'to be' to the ground, in which the tree of philosophy is rooted.
Now since the ground is different from the tree, Heidegger's special
thinking can no longer belong to philosophy, though it is the primary
form of thinking. But what kind of thinking is it then, if it is neither
metaphysics nor philosophy? Heidegger seems to be embarrassed,
and we are quite at a loss as to guess what his real intention is. Does
he want to vanquish metaphysics or does he rather want to protect it?
Is metaphysics the science of being or is it the science of 'to be?' And
what is the science of nothingness? If the metaphysics of being is, as
Heidegger says, the destiny of Europe, whose destiny is the science of
the 'to be' which reveals itself in *Dasein?* And is not the science of

[1] *Einführung*, p. 14 f.
[2] *Kant*, etc., p. 17.
[3] *Was ist Metaphysik?*, p. 39.
[4] *Ibid.*, p. 40.
[5] *Ibid.*, p. 7 f.

nothingness the destiny of the East? I hope that embarrassment is not Heidegger's destiny.

Where will the first thinker to run away from the native land of philosophy, from metaphysics, find his place of rest? For Heidegger, who in spite of his secret nostalgia for religion obstinately refuses to believe in it, presumably through his old ideal of phenomenology and through the influence of Nietzsche's atheism, the only refuge seems to be in poetry. "Philosophy neither rises from science nor does it come out through science. Philosophy is not coordinate with science; it is prior; but not just logically prior or prior in the systematic list of sciences. Philosophy is situated in a quite unique dimension of spiritual existence. Philosophy and its thinking belong to the same order as poetry." [1] What Heidegger here calls philosophy cannot be that traditional metaphysics which engaged in research into being and neglected the problem of the 'to be.' It must be that mystic thinking, the destiny for *Dasein*, that first thinking beyond metaphysics, otherwise the above statement is quite inexplicable. This kind of ambiguity is usual in Heidegger, and makes his thought unduly complicated. At any rate, his thought is obviously an elegy for philosophy, somewhat similar to Bergson's. It may be true that "Singing and thinking are two neighbouring trunks of poetry." [2] But thinking without concepts is certainly not philosophy. Heidegger must admit that. "But since what is like is like only as far as it is different, and since poetry and thinking are most purely alike in that they care about words, the two things are at the same time most apart in their essence. The thinker utters the 'to be,' the poet names what is holy ... We may know something about the relation of philosophy and poetry, but we know nothing of the dialogue between poet and thinker, who dwell near to one another on mountains far apart." [3] Indeed Heidegger may know something about the relation of philosophy to poetry, but unfortunately we cannot understand what it is that he knows. Anyhow if Heidegger has dropped out of the ranks of the philosophers, let us leave him to wander wherever he likes. Perhaps he will haunt the forests and the mountains like a ghost of the Ephesian philosopher uttering mysterious incantations.

The through investigation of Heidegger's philosophy is not our present concern. Still, since his thought is consistently related to the

---

[1] *Einführung*, p. 20.
[2] *Aus der Erfahrung des Denkens*, p. 25.
[3] *Was ist Metaphysik?*, p. 46.

problem of being and metaphysics, the inquiry into Heidegger's concept of metaphysics requires some general assessment of his philosophy. The charm of his philosophy seems to me to depend mainly on his magical terminology. In this respect Heidegger is superior to Bergson. But Heidegger's extraordinary linguistic talent seems to have resulted in confusion of reason rather than illumination of being. This tendency is accelerated by his transition to mysticism and a poetical attitude in his later period, when he loses his earlier phenomenological scientific attitude. In late years Heidegger appears to have been anxious to obscure being rather than to explain it.

The basic tone of Heidegger's thinking in *Sein und Zeit* was subjective idealism. He cleverly evaded the charge of subjective idealism by using concepts like *Dasein* or *Existenz*, which properly imply objective reality, in place of concepts like those of subject, consciousness, or ego. This is just like Bergson's use of the term *image*, to which, though it is an essentially subjective idea, he gave an objective twist, and so filled the gap between idea and reality. Strictly speaking, ontology or metaphysics is possible on the basis of realism. For this philosophy, which pretends itself to be metaphysics and employs realistic concepts like reality and existence, succeeds in covering up its true colours of subjective idealism. For a subjective idealism to admit what is subjective as subjective or what is idealistic as idealistic is contradictory. In this respect, Heidegger is quite consistent. His philosophical position in *Sein und Zeit* was a radical idealism which went so far as to refuse every subjective or idealistic expression.

It is not incorrect, though not the only possible method of metaphysics, to begin the explanation of the 'to be' with the analysis of the ego. This is in fact the accepted method of modern idealism from Descartes to Kant. But, seen from a metaphysical point of view, it was a defect of idealism that it mistook what is prior to us for what is prior in nature. Heidegger himself admitted at first that the analysis of *Dasein* is only the first step of fundamental ontology. But his extraordinary delay in writing the second part, and the fact that in it he finally abandoned the original plan, invited a strong suspicion, for which he had only himself to blame, that he had fallen into subjective idealism. What the analysis of *Dasein* shows is not the truth of being, but the "Shadow in a Cave." The real being reveals itself in the thinking of God. Man can participate in the thinking activity of God only through his reason. The duty of metaphysics is to express this absolute contemplation through conceptual reasoning. Whether this is possible or not, he who denies it must deny metaphysics.

Some remarkable change in his thought, however, seems to have appeared in Heidegger's later works, though Heidegger himself does not admit any essential change. He explains the turn (*Kehr*) – which may imply his recent change – as being only methodological and already presupposed in *Sein und Zeit*, in which his fundamental ontology was characterised as the preliminary part of the whole ontology. Nevertheless, this change did not form the second volume of *Sein und Zeit*, but was only suggested in an extremely unsatisfactory form in his lectures. And this is inconsistent with its being already allowed for in the original plan.

The most essential and conspicuous change is the interpretation of *Existenz* as *Ek-sistenz*. In *Ueber den Humanismus*, this term is explained as meaning that *Dasein* or man stands outside himself in the light of the 'to be.' [1] In *Sein und Zeit* Heidegger said that there is 'to be,' as far as there is *Dasein*. [2] But his new theory is on the contrary that "the 'to be' is given to man as far as the illumination of the 'to be' takes place." [3] He also explains that the word *Da*, which implies the illumination of the 'to be' emerges as the destiny or dispensation (*Schickung*) of the 'to be' itself; to prove this he quotes the following from *Sein und Zeit:* "to be is absolute transcendence." [4] But here Heidegger is guilty of distortion. In its original context this word only meant the transcendence of the 'to be' from mere being, not transcendence from a subject as now explained.

Anyhow, according to the later thought in the letter on Humanism, the 'to be' illuminates itself towards human being in its *ekstatic* i.e. outstanding projection (*Entwurf*) but this projection itself does not make the 'to be.' Besides, this projection is at the same time 'thrownness' (*Geworfenheit*); he who projects in this projection is not the man, but the 'to be' itself. [5] "Man is not the master of being, but its shepherd." [6] "Man is, from his essence in the history of the 'to be,' such a being, whose way of being consists in *Ek-sistenz*, i.e. in living near the 'to be.' Man is the neighbour of the 'to be.' " *Existenz* is "fundamentally different from all realities, living near the 'to be,'

---

[1] *Humanismus*, pp. 66 ff. (Franckes Ausg.).
[2] *Sein und Zeit*, p. 212.
[3] *Humanismus*, p. 83.
[4] *Sein und Zeit*, p. 38.
[5] *Humanismus*, p. 84.
[6] *Ibid.*, p. 90.

outside oneself. Watching (the to be); in other words, interested in the 'to be.'" [1]

"Man is projected, by the 'to be,' in the truth of the 'to be.' Consequently, he watches the truth of the 'to be,' and thereby stands outside himself, in such a way that being appears as what actually is, in the light of the 'to be.' [2] "Man does not decide whether it appears or not, or how it appears, whether God or gods, history or nature comes in the illumination of the 'to be,' whether it exists or is passing away, or how it does so. The coming of the 'to be' depends upon the destiny (Geschick) of the 'to be.'" [3]

Heidegger's recent thought cannot be simply characterised as a subjective idealism, for to admit the transcendence of being, if not of the 'to be,' is essential to realism and metaphysics. But, then, is there any change in his thought about the distinction between being and the 'to be,' metaphysics and the thinking about the 'to be,'? We have already mentioned Heidegger's oscillation with regard to the opposition between metaphysics and ontology. If the 'to be' is transcendence, and its illumination is the projection of the 'to be' by itself, the 'to be' apart from *Dasein* will be obscured, since it is lacking in *Da*, in which it can reveal itself. But though obscured, it is not necessarily non-existent. The 'to be' is more than the appearance of being towards *Dasein*. Then, how does the thinking of the 'to be' reveal and explain the 'to be?' Heidegger's answer is astonishingly simple: *Es ist es selbst* [4] – it is itself. Indeed, how extraordinary that human Reason should be intoxicated with such an empty and mocking statement? I feel that I have glimpsed the destiny of the German nation, the abyss of sin, into which this most intellectual people is apt to fall. I hope that Heidegger's mysticism and Hitler's fanaticism are not the neighbours who "dwell near to one another on mountains far apart."

The simplicity of the answer, *Es ist es selbst* is not inferior to Parmenides' great *Anfang*. And the return to the beginning is for Heidegger, without doubt, an honourable destiny. But this is a complete refusal to accept the progress of knowledge, a decisive manifestation of a retrogressive spirit. If the thinking of the 'to be' leads to this tautology, it proves that thinking in this manner is not suitable for cognition. Notwithstanding these difficulties, Heidegger repeats his earlier polemic against metaphysics, as if nothing had happened.

[1] *Ibid.*, p. 91.
[2] *Ibid.*, p. 75.
[3] *Ibid.*, p. 75.
[4] *Ibid.*, p. 76.

"When thinking thinks of being *qua* being, it is actually related to the 'to be.' But in fact it thinks the being *qua* being, and never thinks the 'to be' *qua* 'to be.' The question of the 'to be' remains always a question of being ... the truth of the 'to be' as illumination itself remains closed to metaphysics." [1] "Not only did metaphysics not raise the question as to the truth of the 'to be,' it raised the wrong questions insofar as metaphysics remains in ignorance of the 'to be.' " [2] In the days of *Sein und Zeit*, when ontology was the inquiry into the 'to be' and was the phenomenological disclosure of the 'to be' through the analysis of *Dasein* as human being, this word was welcome as suggesting the dawn of a new philosophy. But now when the thinking of the 'to be' has come to obscure the 'to be' instead of disclosing it, this word has become quite disillusioning.

---

[1] *Ibid.*, p. 76 f.
[2] *Ibid.*, p. 93.

CHAPTER VI

THE LOGICAL POSITIVISTS' VIEW
OF METAPHYSICS

The main aim of the school[1] sometimes called logical positivism, and later rather called neo-positivism, was without doubt to free philosophy from metaphysics. It is all the more astonishing to find that neither the definition nor the historical investigation of the concept "metaphysics" has ever been undertaken seriously in this school. Ayer for instance, in his famous anti-metaphysical work, "Language, Truth, and Logic",[2] says, "We are not now concerned with the historical question how much of what has traditionally passed for philosophy is actually metaphysical." What must be noticed here is that his lack of interest in this historical question is an essential and fundamental trait of this school rather than a temporal reservation. But I wonder what significance there is in denying metaphysics without giving an explicit definition to the term "metaphysics." Although Ayer stated in that context that he would offer a definition later, this promise has, to all appearances, not been fulfilled. If, however, this definition may be suggested in such sentences as "We may accordingly define a metaphysical sentence as a sentence which purports to express a genuine proposition, but does, in fact, express neither a tautology nor an empirical hypothesis",[3] or "Being metaphysical, it is neither true nor

---

[1] There is a question as to the extension of this denomination.
In the narrowest sense, it is confined to the Vienna Circle or even to part of this school. In this strict sense, even Wittgenstein, who was practically the founder of this school, should be excluded. After the death of Moritz Schlick, its leader, the school was led by Carnap, while Reichenbach gradually departed from the orthodox tendency. The deviation is more remarkable in the case of Popper. Perhaps Ayer is the most unfailing advocate of this school. The most respectable mark of this school is the criticism among its members, which is an exceptional phenomenon in philosophical circles. Our criticism, therefore, is sufficiently attained by tracing the controversies among the members themselves.

[2] Ayer, A. J., *Language, Truth and Logic*. 1936. 2ed. 1946. p. 41.

[3] *Ibid.*

false but literally senseless,"[1] we must conclude that this is neither a definition, nor an empirical summary, but a sheer slander of metaphysics.[2]

From these considerations it seems to me as though the logical positivists would not take the name of metaphysics as anything but mere verbiage. Once a metaphysical sentence is thus defined as a nonsensical sentence, it is evident enough that the negation of metaphysics follows without any criticism. For instead of inquiring whether or not metaphysics is meaningful, they simply call what is nonsensical metaphysics. From such a dogmatic supposition it is a matter of course that there has been no interest in determining what part of the historical theories of philosophy should be taken as metaphysics. But is it really plausible that every kind of traditional metaphysics should have existed only to be ridiculed by Ayer and his fellows?

Moritz Schlick, the chief of the Vienna Circle, and the founder of logical positivism, was one of the few exceptional positivists who have dealt with the concept of metaphysics with some sobriety, though even his study was very unsatisfactory from either the historical or the logical point of view. In his early treatise, "Erlebnis, Erkenntnis, Metaphysik,"[3] Schlick took up first for investigation an interpretation of metaphysics as indirect knowledge of transcendent beings through concepts. According to him, this is in fact a characteristic of knowledge in general not peculiar to metaphysics. All knowledge, he says, is indirect and is mediated with symbols. Therefore, if metaphysics be so interpreted, it is only too evident that metaphysics is possible.[4] But a definition more proper to metaphysics, according to Schlick, is "intuition of transcendent objects." Schopenhauer, for instance, explains that metaphysics inspects the inside of a building, while other sciences walk around the building and sketch its façade from every point of view. According to Bergson, similarly, science only copies an object through the symbols of spatial form, while the activity of philosophy, i.e. metaphysical investigation, is to interject oneself in terms of intuition into the core of the object. Though these explanations require for metaphysics special means of knowledge, viz. intuition *sui generis*,[5] Schlick himself rejects this supposition, saying that

[1] *Ibid.* p. 31.
[2] Hence Main's ironic query as to whether Ayer's proposition is suitable to "Mind" or to "Mercury."
[3] Schlick, M., *Erleben, Erkennen, Metaphysik.* Kant Studien XXXI. 1926.
[4] *Ibid.* 147 ff.
[5] *Ibid.* 155 f.

intuitional knowledge is a *contradictio in adjecto*. "In so far as the meta-physician requires experience," Schlick argues, "his requirement will be fulfilled, only in the sense that one can promote the richness of consciousness through poetry, the arts, and life itself. Whereas when the metaphysician wants to experience transcendent beings, he con-fuses thereby life with knowledge and seeks for a vain illusion. Trans-cendent beings can be recognized, but cannot be experienced. The system of a metaphysician sometimes contains knowledge and poetry, but no metaphysics."[1]

In short, Schlick pointed out two views of metaphysics, viz., that which takes it as the conceptual knowledge of transcendent objects, and that which takes it as the intuitional experience of the same ob-jects. The former was rejected by Schlick because it is rather appropri-ate to science in general, while the latter was rejected because it in-volves contradiction and is therefore impossible. Thus the task of meta-physicians was assumed by him to be a kind of experience like poetry. But I wonder what kind of existence it is the experience of, if not the experience of transcendent objects. Is it instead an expression of sub-jective emotion under the guise of knowledge of objects? Be that as it may, what is the difference between metaphysics and poetry? It may be answered that poetry is the expression of emotion in terms of ideas, while metaphysics uses concepts. Then, is it that concepts as well as ideas are subjective phenomena irrelevant to transcendent objects? To these problems no distinct answer was given by Schlick.

With regard to the first definition presented by Schlick, it is no doubt unsatisfactory for the definition of metaphysics. We are not sure from whom this definition is derived, but whoever he may be, he should at least have distinguished metaphysics from other sciences. Either he should have indicated under transcendent objects something different from what was meant by Schlick, viz., the object of science in general, or he should have implied by knowledge something more than what was implied by Schlick. Granting that metaphysics is the knowledge of transcendent objects, there still remains the question of what this transcendent means. Is it that the object of metaphysics is over and beyond common intellect including the intellect of scientists, or is it that the object cannot be perceived by our senses? In making all know-ledge refer to transcendents, Schlick appears to have distinguished the object of knowledge from the content of experience. The content of experience is *per se* a mental phenomenon, but the object of knowledge

[1] *Ibid.* 158.

exists outside the mind, either as the cause of this mental phenomenon or as the end at which it aims. Whereas the object of metaphysics is transcendent means not that it exists outside the mind,
but that it is beyond sense-experience, and therefore constitutes the
object of conceptual thinking.[1] Although Schlick identified transcendent objects with objects in general, we don't know a single philosopher who ever has made such an identification. If metaphysics were
the knowledge of objects in general, what kind of knowledge is science
proper but knowledge without an object – an astonishing conclusion
even for a metaphysician?

It is true that Kant regarded dogmatic metaphysics as having pur-
ported knowledge of things-in-themselves. At first glance this conception of the old metaphysics is in some respect akin to the first definition of metaphysics by Schlick. But there is a remarkable distinction
between Kant's concept of things-in-themselves and Schlick's concept
of object. An object is recognized, but a thing-in-itself is *ex hypothesi*
unrecognizable. According to Kant, the object of science is phenomena, while according to Schlick, phenomena are immanent to mind and
cannot be the object of science. What is threatened by Schlick's concept of phenomena is therefore empirical science rather than metaphysics. Metaphysics defined as the knowledge of objects is obviously
possible, while science could not be knowledge because it is to be concerned only with phenomena. In fact, Kant never overlooked the
"intentional" function of consciousness, at least with regard to scientific knowledge. There is no cognition without an object. It was because Kant required for knowledge sense-intuition as its constituent
that he regarded transcendent being as unrecognizable, though it can
be thought of. Transcendent being, the object of dogmatic metaphysics
before Kant, was pure intelligible object. With regard to such an
object Kant denied the possibility of knowledge in the strict sense.
It may be thought of, but cannot be known. For thinking, pure intellect is sufficient, but for knowing, sense-intuition is additionally
required. This distinction between knowledge and thinking is common
to Kant and the empiricists.

According to Schlick, the transcendent is the object of knowledge
rather than the content of experience, while intuition is a kind of

---

[1] For example, Carnap explains in a note (1957) to his "Elimination," that
the word "metaphysics" is used in that paper, as usually in Europe, for the field
of alleged knowledge of the essence of things which transcends the realm of
empirically founded, inductive science.

experience rather than knowledge. It follows therefore that meta-physics as intuition of the transcendent is impossible. But it is doubt-ful whether we can distinguish intuition from knowledge so strictly. Intuition is usually understood as direct perception of an object; to limit it to the sensuous is a thought peculiar to Kant. By intuition of the transcendent, metaphysicians generally mean non-sensuous in-tuition, and whether intuition of the transcendent is impossible is a matter for further investigation. In the concept of intuition itself there is nothing that prevents its being non-sensuous and intellectual. As far as a corporeal object is concerned, the direct perception of it would be sensuous without doubt. But if there be any intelligible object what-soever, the direct perception of it, if possible, can by no means be sen-suous. Is there then really no intelligible and non-sensible object at all? In respect to this point the criticism of the positivists is restricted to general and abstract concepts,[1] though there might be some ques-tion whether they are all what are called intelligible objects. In any case, these concepts are excluded by the positivists from the region of being as mere logical fictions or psychological phenomena. But if not real, at least they are the objects of logic and psychology without doubt. Then, how is it possible for these objects and the perception of such objects to be of pure sensible character? One might argue that they are at least of sensible origin inasmuch as they are derived from the experience of individual beings. Still the objects of traditional metaphysics such as God, freedom, and mind seem to belong to a different order. The concept of God is neither a general name for indi-vidual gods nor an abstraction from concrete gods. Even if the concept of mind may be formed from individual minds, there must be presup-posed the existence of some such minds, and an existing mind cannot be a sensible object. In fact, the concept of mind is something more than a logical generalization of particular mental phenomena. The mind is, so to say, a *noetic* synthesis, just as the body is a *noematic* synthesis, of mental phenomena. It is rather a collective term than a general name. And the formation of such a collective term is regulated, in the last analysis, by a teleological principle. Thus if the concept of mind is false, so also is the concept of body, and we shall be led to pan-pheno-menalism, which admits no synthetic unity of phenomena. This, how-ever, is not the necessary result of positivism.

[1] Carnap, R., "Empiricism, Semantics, and Ontology," *Revue Internationale de Philosophie.* II. (1950) p. 33. repr. in *Semantics and the Philosophy of Language.* p. 221.

Take for example other concepts of a more empirical character such as person, nation, and state. I admit that concept and existence are not the same. But the concept has two sides. From one point of view, it is a kind of idea as a mental phenomenon, but from another point of view, it is the object of this idea. We have in mind the idea of person, we use the concept of person in our judgement, but person *per se* is neither an idea nor a concept as a mere part of judgement; it is an object, an object of our knowledge as well as of our conduct. Now, may we not infer that there is vision with which we see a state or a person, just as there is vision with which we see a flower? Such vision, if any, should be called intellectual intuition. Further, with regard to value, it must be distinguished from evaluation. The sense of value is of course an activity of a mind or of a person, whereas the value itself is attributed to an object rather than to the mind which finds that object to be valuable. So, if the value should be regarded as subjective because of the sense of value being a kind of feeling, for the same reason colour should be regarded as belonging not to an object but to a subject, since the sense of colour is obviously a mental activity. And this is, as is well known, the final issue of the empiricists' theory of knowledge. But it seems to me more desirable to admit intelligible objects analogous to sensible objects with some reservation. God, mind, person, state, and many kinds of value do not exist in the same way as corporeal objects, but they are none the less objects of knowledge and being objects, they must be perceived by our intellectual intuition.

Thus, there is only a single alternative: either we ought to deny every object, or we ought to admit both sensible and intelligible objects. But the first case leads to absurdity, because it will require feeling or experience without any corresponding object. We might rather say that even subjective feeling is related to some object.

The alleged distinction between experience and knowledge is possible only in the German language which has the two concepts *Erlebnis* and *Erfahrung*. In ordinary language, the one means emotional and subjective experience, while the other means rational and objective experience; the one consists mainly of sense-intuition, while the other involves both sensuous and intellectual elements. Now, it is the tendency of conceptualism to oppose intuition and cognition. According to Kant, cognition consists of intuition and thinking, and thinking without intuition is not adequate for knowledge in the strict sense. Hence Kant considered that metaphysics cannot be the system of knowledge inasmuch as it lacks intuition of its proper objects. This is really an unavoidable result if intuition is confined to sense-perception. But it is otherwise when intellectual intuition is assumed possible. Kant never showed why our intuition should be confined to the sensuous; instead he only defined the sense as the faculty of receiving representation through being affected by an object.[1] From this definition it is a matter of course that every intuition is of sensuous character. That sense is passive and intellect is active was Kant's dogmatic assumption, which automatically ruled out intellectual intuition of any kind.

As for Schlick, it is unlikely that he restricted intuition to the sensuous. He rather maintained that metaphysics as a science is impossible on the ground that if metaphysical objects were perceived directly, they would form experience rather than thinking. For thinking, according to Schlick, has to be mediated by symbols. This inference by Schlick, however, does not follow of necessity, because there is room for metaphysics to be formed through the combination of intellectual intuition and conceptual thinking through symbols. All traditional metaphysics was constituted of these two kinds of faculty, not of either intuition or thinking exclusively.

Several years later Schlick again took up the problem of metaphysics in a short treatise called "Positivism and Realism."[2] In this treatise, he says that he is a positivist insofar as positivism signifies the negation of metaphysics. But the meaning of metaphysics, according to him, is different from that which is generally used in philosophical literature. This amounts to saying that he did not deny metaphysics in its ordinary sense, and that therefore he was not a positivist in the usual sense. But as to the special meaning of metaphysics in which he denied metaphysics Schlick gave no explanation. This is quite a pity.

On the other hand, however, Schlick explained the usual meaning of metaphysics adopted by the Eleatics, Plato, and every later metaphysician, viz., it is the theory of "true being," of "reality in itself," or of "transcendent being." Now, these beings are opposed to spurious, less, or apparent being respectively. Apparent being is phenomena, but real and transcendent being is to be attained only by the effort of metaphysicians. Special sciences, on the other hand, only undertake the investigation of phenomena which are acceptable to them. If it were the case that the positivists' rejection of metaphysics consists in

[1] Kant, I., *K. d. r. V. Tr. Aesth*. I. 1.
[2] Positivismus und Realismus. 1932–33. Eng. tr. in *Synthese* 1848–49. Log. Pos. 1959.

the denial of transcendent being, it would follow that the positivists admit only non-transcendent being, viz., what is given to them. According to Schlick, some positivists really held this contention, but they made thereby a metaphysical proposition to the same extent as those who maintained the existence of transcendent being. If a philosopher considers that he may talk only about what is given to him, he is a solipsistic metaphysician, and when he considers that what is given is distributed among many subjects, he is a kind of Berkeleian. In such an interpretation, positivism is identical with the old idealistic metaphysics. But since what the founder of positivism sought for was not the restoration of idealism, such an interpretation must be rejected as contrary to the antimetaphysical attitude of positivism.[1] So argues Schlick.

Schlick himself admits that his philosophy belongs, in a sense, to positivism, but he distinguishes it from the old positivism calling his own "logical positivism", or "consistent empiricism." According to his explanation, it never makes such an assertion as that only what is given is existent; for such an assertion is nonsense. A consistent empiricist does not deny the existence of the outside world, he only points out the empirical meaning of existential propositions. The logical positivist is not opposed to realism; the opposition exists only between the consistent empiricist and the metaphysician. The logical positivist is opposed to both realistic and idealistic metaphysicians. To deny the existence of the outside world is as much a metaphysical proposition as to affirm it. The consistent empiricist regards both affirmation and negation to be meaningless. To say that statements about the metaphysical outside world are meaningless is quite different from saying that the outside world does not exist. The empiricist does not say to the metaphysician that he is wrong, but that what he says does not form an assertion. The empiricist does not oppose the metaphysician; he says, "I don't understand you."[2] Thus explains Schlick.

In short, what Schlick calls metaphysics is any assertion whatsoever with regard to the existence of an object rather than the knowledge of transcendent being, and the last issue of logical positivism is an *epoche* of judgement with regard to the existence and non-existence of an object. Compared with traditional terminology, Schlick's first conception to the effect that metaphysics deals with the existence and non-existence of an object seems to agree with ontology or *metaphysica*

[1] *Ibid.* (Log. Pos.) p. 85.
[2] *Ibid.* 1–6 f.

generalis, and the second one which makes metaphysics refer to trans-cendent being seems to coincide with natural theology as a part of *metaphysica specialis.* With regard to this second concept, as we have said above, what was meant by transcendent being was the intelligible object rather than the object in general. In assuming in this treatise the transcendent to be the object of metaphysics, Schlick appears to have approached one step closer to the traditional concept.

We now come to understand the meaning of metaphysics which Schlick at first avoided giving: it is to affirm or to deny the reality of the outside world, to ask the question as to the being of things. A strange coincidence between Heidegger and Schlick can be found here with regard to the concept of metaphysics; both of them regard tradi-tional metaphysics as having been concerned with the existence and non-existence of things. They depart however from one another in that the one presents a new question "What is it to be?"[1] distinguished from the question of what exists, whereas the other rejects the question of being decisively. Schlick in his treatise did not touch on Heidegger, but taking into account the fact that Carnap in his "Elimination of Metaphysics," which appeared in the same year as Schlick's treatise, criticized the philosophy of Heidegger as an example of metaphysical nonsense, it is highly probable that for Schlick also Heidegger's new theory offered a motive for his argument. [2]

In this last mentioned treatise,[3] Carnap attributed the error in making pseudo-proposition to the logical misuse of the word "to be." This word is sometimes used as a copula, for example when we say, "I am hungry." But sometimes it is also used to express existence, as for example, when we say, "I am." Metaphysics, so says Carnap, often did not understand the ambiguity of this word, and confused being as a verb-form with existence, and thus it turned out that they were re-duced to pseudo- propositions like 'I am" or "God is." In Descartes' *"Cogito ergo sum,"* for instance, *sum* is usually taken to imply the existence of *ego.* But according to Carnap, reality should be used with some predicate and it is wrong to use it with a subject. The proposition

---

[1] Heidegger, M., *Was ist Metaphysik?* p. 7 f. Einführung in die Metaphysik p. 14 f.

[2] Heidegger's *Was ist Metaphysik* appeared in 1929, *Sein und Zeit,* in 1927, while Schlick's *Positivismus und Realismus* appeared in 1932.

[3] Carnap, R., *Ueberwindung der Metaphysik durch Logische Analyse der Sprhcae.* Erkenntnis. Vo. II. (1932) Eng. tr. The Elimination of Metaphysics Through Logical Analysis of Language. in Log. Pos. p. 73 f. cf. Schlick, *op. cit.* p. 98.

which expresses reality must be "There exists something of such and such a kind" instead of "A exists." It was also wrong, continues Carnap, for Descartes to infer "I exist" from "I think." If an existential proposition is to be deduced from the proposition P(a), i.e., from the proposition "a posesses the attribute P," then the existence should be asserted in respect to the predicated P instead of to the subject a. What follows from "I think" is not "I am," but "There exists something that thinks."

Carnap's real intention was not, however, to explain the existence of an object, but to maintain that only copulative "be" is significant. The same issue was brought up by Ayer[1] after several years. Ayer argued that it was a mistake from the apparent resemblance of grammatical form between "Martyrs suffer" and "Martyrs exist" that one thought to be able to think about the being of martyrs, though these two sentences are not the same in their logical character. This remark of Ayer's is not, however, a new idea as it might appear, for it is already implied in Kant's statement to the effect that existence is a *Posit* instead of a real predicate. Kant implied therewith that this statement involved no expansion of knowledge, just as the positivists considered Descartes' statement "I am" to involve no knowledge. It involves no knowledge, to be sure. But is there no significance at all? He who says "I am conscious" is not the same as he who says nothing. The content of his consciousness is not expressed in this sentence, still it is implied none the less.

To resume Schlick's argument, it is worthy of special attention that Schlick distinguished two meanings of the term "outside world."[2] The one is the outside world in its usual sense, which is the same as what is called "nature" by physicists. The other is the outside world of the metaphysicians which signifies transcendent being *par excellence*, viz., that which is over and beyond the empirical world. This distinction, according to Schlick, is due to past philosophers' view that required direct perception in order to recognize an object. Those philosophers regarded that what cannot be directly experienced or perceived remains unknowable, incomprehensible, transcendent, and belongs to the realm of things-in-themselves. Schlick considered that the error in this conception lay in the confusion of knowledge and acquaintance or experience in his special terminology, according to which experience was equivalent to *Erlebnis* distinguished from *Erfahrung*. As we have

[1] Ayer, A. J., Language, *Truth and Logic.* 1936. rev. ed. 1946. Ch. I. p. 42.
[2] Pos. & Rea. p. 100 f.

pointed out elsewhere, this conception of Schlick's, however, is incon-sistent for an empiricist who usually identifies knowledge with ex-perience.

It is doubtful moreover whether, as Schlick considered, most of the past philosophers required immediate perception in order to know an object. As far as perception is literally taken as sensuous faculty, this was surely not the case. Again, if the notion of perception contains intellectual as well as sensuous intuition, most of the past philosophers did not admit that there is anything which cannot be perceived by this faculty. Schlick himself mentioned Schopenhauer and Bergson as representatives of the metaphysicians who considered that the object of metaphysics was to be perceived by this kind of intellectual intuition. The metaphysical outside world is transcendent of sense-experience, to be sure. But this does not amount to saying that it transcends experience in general, much less does it mean that it is inconceivable. Therefore, it was not most of past philosophers but Kant and his empiri-cal followers who regarded transcendent being as utterly inconceivable.

According to the early Carnap,[1] who made a frontal attack upon metaphysics, the development of modern logic made it possible to give a new and sharper answer to the question of the validity and justifica-tion of metaphysics. "The researches of applied logic or the theory of knowledge, which aim at clarifying the cognitive content of scientific statements lead to a positive and negative result. The positive result is worked out in the domain of empirical science; the various concepts of the branches of science are clarified; their formal logical and episto-emological connections are made explicit. In the domain of meta-physics, including all philosophy of value and normative theory, logical analysis yields the negative result that the alleged statements in this domain are entirely meaningless. Therewith a radical elimination of metaphysics is attained, which was not yet possible from the earlier antimetaphysical standpoints." So argued Carnap. But it is doubtful how such a result could be attained without supposing the explicit definition of metaphysics and the comprehensive classification of metaphysical propositions. In fact, the positivists' criticism of meta-physics was nothing but a dogmatic interpretation of some propo-sitions chosen at random from some philosophers whom they did not like. It is natural therefore that Carnap's radical elimination of meta-physics should provoke controversy even within the same school.

[1] Carnap. R., *Elimination* etc. p. 60 f.

Whether or not to support this attitude of Carnap's was the mark by which logical positivists were distinguished from other analytical philosophers of more moderate tendency.

In Feigl's "Logical Empiricism,"[1] which appeared in 1943, the indiscriminate criticism of metaphysics was replaced by a far more discreet view. Feigl made an apology for positivism, saying that its criticism of metaphysics was primarily an attack upon the confusion of meanings and was not intended as a wholesale repudiation of what had been presented under that label. Whether or not Feigl's explanation fits the original intention of the positivists, it was certainly the fact that such a wholesale repudiation did not succeed. Traditional metaphysics would never fall under such an attack. A criticism without any clear-cut definition of the term could by no means attain the aim even if it really wanted to. Feigl rightly noticed the variety of metaphysical theories, but what he presented was neither historical investigation nor definition of metaphysics, but only an incomplete enumeration of the methods of metaphysics. With regard to the term "metaphysics," Feigl is content with the common understanding "the theory of first principles" or "the theory of the whole of existence." With this supposition Feigl proceeds to classify metaphysical methods as intuitive, deductive, dialectical, transcendental, and inductive. Each of these methods was subjected to precise criticism. In the first place, "inductive metaphysics is a speculative cosmology derived by extrapolation from scientific evidence and scientific theory," and "this needs not contain factually meaningless elements at all." "Metaphysics in this sense, though logically unasailable, is open to criticism from the point of view of the criteria of adequacy and precision, reliability and fruitfulness. Conjectures regarding the heat-death of the universe, the origin or life, and the future of evolution may be perfectly meaningful, but anyone with a superficial acquaintance with scientific method will realize how uncertain and vague these guesses must be. Occasionally they may be valuable suggestions for further research, but with the exception of a few notable instances like the ancient atomic hypothesis, they are apt to remain barren, if not actually misleading. Inductive metaphysics is thus merely the risky, sanguine, disreputable extreme of science."

In the second place, "deductive metaphysics indulges in the ratio-

1 Feigl. H., *Logical Empiricism* in *Twentieth Century Philosophy*. D. D. Runes, ed. Philosoph. Library, Nr. 1943. repr. in *Readings in Philosophical Analysis*. 1949. p. 11 f.

nalistic practice of producing factual conclusions of a relatively specific character from a few sweepingly general premises, and thus misconstrues the nature of logical derivation, and is guilty of a confusion of logical with factual meaning." In the third place, "dialectical metaphysics, especially the Hegelian, confuses what may appear as a psychological thought movement or as a form of historical processes with the logical forms of inference." In the fourth place, "intuitive metaphysics convinced of the existence of a privileged shortcut to 'truth', mistakes having an experience for knowing something about it. Then, too, it is habitually insensitive to the distinction between pictorial and emotional appeals and factual meaning.

In the fifth place and finally, "transcendental metaphysics in its attempt to uncover the basic categories of both thought and reality may turn out to be nothing else than an unclear combination of epistemology and cosmology, which is then dignified with the name "ontology." It could thus be salvaged and restated in purified form. But it is precisely in ontology that we find the greatest accumulation of factually meaningless verbiage. Speculations concerning the "absolute," even if not entirely devoid of "empirical components," generally contain ample measure of "absolutely" untestable pseudo-propositions. The customary excuse that further experience or reasoning will validate these ideas has no bearing on the question of meaningfulness. What the most patient empiricist can do here is to hope that doubtful promises to define empirically the terms used so far only emotively will sometime be fulfilled. But until that happens, the empiricist will fail to attach any glimmering of factual-meaning to the metaphysics which rotates about these terms." This is a summary of Feigl's criticism of metaphysics.

The canon of meaningfulness we shall investigate later. Feigl's criticism may partly fit some metaphysical theories, but it is not valid for metaphysics in general. His argument is not sufficient insofar as it depends upon incomplete enumeration of metaphysical methods, and the object of criticism also remains ambiguous. For instance, in the case of dialectical metaphysics, to condemn it for the confusion of historical facts and the forms of logical inference does not do away with Hegelianism, which willingly assumes the basic identity of history and logic. The problem will finally turn out how cognition of history is possible if fact and logic are to be simply separated from each other. With regard to transcendental metaphysics, even if, as Feigl says, ontology contains some pseudo-propositions, it does not make ontology absolutely impossible. The barrenness of empirical metaphysics is not proved successfully either. It is not wonderful therefore that even among analytical philosophers there are some who regard the distinction between scientific hypothesis and metaphysical theory to be merely relative.[1]

The logical positivist erred inexcusably in wanting to eliminate metaphysics without making an explicit definition of metaphysics. Evading the painstaking work of historical investigation, they simply neglected metaphysics instead of criticizing it. Kraft[2] differentiated the past task of philosophers into three forms. The first was the problem of empirical fact, and this was answered by empirical science. The second was the problem of description and language, which was explained by the rationale of concepts and statements. The third was the problem of metaphysics, and this could not be expressed through scientific terms and concepts. Thus, from the historical domain of philosophy, the first part was purged, and there remained only the second part. Thus philosophy would be restricted to logic. Now, description and language have their proper object, but the relation between descriptive language and its object is not the object of pure logic. It will be separated from syntax and forms, as semantics, an independent branch of logic. With regard to Kraft's words, however, we are unsure what it means to say that there are metaphysical problems which cannot be expressed in scientific terms. If there are problems at all, is it not the duty of philosophers to devise scientific terms for them? For what reason does he deny the possibility of scientific expression of such problems? The inability of past metaphysicians is not a sufficient reason to deny the possibility of metaphysics. The logical positivists simply ignored the possibility without making any effort. They declared arrogantly that an insoluble problem is no problem at all. Wittgenstein,[3] for example, says: "It is not to be wondered at that the deepest problems are no problems." (4.003) "For an answer which cannot be expressed, the question too cannot be expressed. The riddle does not exist. If a question can be put at all, then it can also be answered." (6.5) "Scepticism is not irrefutable, but palpably senseless, if it would doubt where a question cannot be asked. For doubt can only exist where there is a question; and a question only where there is an answer, and this only where something can be said." (6.51), therefore, "Where-

---

[1] Popper, K. R., *Conjectures and Refutations*. 1963. p. 257.
[2] Kraft, V., *Der Wiener Kreis*. 1950 P. 175.
[3] Wittgenstein, L., *Tractatus Logico-Philosophicus*. 1922.

of one cannot speak, thereof one must be silent." It seems to me as if he were a physician who would neglect the existence of patient whom he cannot cure, saying "He whom I cannot cure, is not a patient at all."

Obviously there is in the ground of the logical positivists' contention some antipathy and horror regarding metaphysics. It is this ill-feeling that makes them neglect the historical investigation of metaphysics. To avoid Bradley's paradox[1] to the effect that anyone who grants as impossible such knowledge as metaphysics asserts a *de facto* metaphysical proposition, Wittgenstein tried to determine that which is unthinkable from that which is thinkable.[2] It was all the more ironical that in spite of such desperate effort Wittgenstein was obliged[3] to admit that his proposition had no meaning.

As was said above, Schlick[4] boldly maintained: "The logical positivist does not contradict metaphysics." Whether we ought to regard this lack of understanding as a lack of intelligence or as a lack of interest differs according to our viewpoint. But the logical positivist must at least give some justification for his indifference, for to say that something is meaningless is not the same as to say that he is indifferent to it. The former implies that his indifference is justified, while the latter states only the fact of one's personal disposition. To say that what the metaphysician says is meaningless, is evidently an attack against the metaphysician, unlike such a statement as "I am a chemist and you are a philosopher" or "I am only interested in chemistry and am indifferent to philosophy."

Popper[5] nicely pointed out the secret of logical positivism when he said: "Nothing is so easy as revealing a problem to be a meaningless pseudo problem. For that purpose one only determine the notion of meaning narrowly enough; in this way one may explain every difficult problem so as to find it empty of meaning. And, on the other hand, one is to admit only science as being meaningful. Further, every argument about the notion of meaning turns out to be meaningless. That is, once enthroned, this dogma would, as Wittgenstein said in the preface to his book, become invincible and definitive." Indeed, the procedure of the logical positivist is like that of Procrustes. He has a bed of

[1] Bradley, F. H., *Appearance and Reality* 1.
[2] Wittgenstein, *op. cit.* (4, 114).
[3] *Ibid.* (6. 54)
[4] Cf. note 15.
[5] Popper, *Logik der Forschung.* 1935 p. 21.

meaningfulness and cuts everybody's leggs under the name of meta-physical nonsense. Disregarding every desire of the metaphysician, the logical positivist indulges himself in polishing his bed of "meaningful-ness."

Wittgenstein is said to have been the first to set up the measure of meaningfulness in verification. What is most likely to indicate the issue in the *Tractatus*[1] runs: "But to be able to say that a point is black or white, I must first know under what conditions a point is called white or black; in order to be able to say "p" is true, (or false) I must have determined under what conditions I call "p" true, and thereby I determine the sense of the proposition." – A rather redundant passage for the *Tractatus* which makes terseness its principle. This thought was more elaborated by Schlick and Carnap.

In "Positivism and Realism" Schlick formulated meaningfulness as follows:[2] "Every proposition has meaning only insofar as it can be verified, and it says only what is verified and simply nothing more." "A proposition only has meaning, is verifiable, only if I can state the conditions under which it would be true and under which it would be false."[3] "A proposition has a statable meaning only if it makes a verifiable difference whether it is true or false."[4] Schlick went so far as to identify the meaning of a proposition with its verification. He says for instance: "The statement of the conditions under which a pro-position is true is the same as the statement of its meaning, and not something different."[5] In "Meaning and Verification,"[6] which was published in the year of his violent death, he said: "stating the mean-ing of a sentence amounts to stating the rules according to which the sentence is to be used, and this is the same as stating the way in which it can be verified (or falsified)." There follows the famous statement: "The meaning of a proposition is the method of its verification."

Now, verification means stating the conditions under which a pro-position or statement is true or false, or in other words, by the exami-nation of sense-experience, as Schlick put it: "In order to find the meaning of a proposition, we must transform it by successive defini-

[1] Wittgenstein, *op. cit.* (4.063)
[2] Schlick, *op. cit.* p. 90.
[3] *Ibid.* 98 f.
[4] *Ibid.* 88
[5] *Ibid.* p. 87.
[6] Schlick, "Meaning and Verification." *The Philoslphical Review* 45, 1436. repr. in R. Ph. A. p. 148.

tions until finally only such words occur in it as can no longer be defined, but whose meaning can only be directly pointed out."[1] "And
these conditions, ... must finally be discoverable in the given. The
meaning of every proposition is finally to be determined by the given,
and by nothing else."[2] "for verifiable certainly means nothing but
capable of being exhibited in the given."[3] "There is no way of understanding any meaning without ultimate reference to ostensive definitions, and this means, in an obvious sense, reference to experience or
possibility of verification."[4] Carnap made explicit that this experience
is of a sensuous character; as he put it: "All concepts used in the science
could be defined on the basis of observational or perceptual experience,"[5] or "a string of words has meaning only if its derivability relations from protocol sentences (observation sentences) are given ..."[6]

Lewis[7] and Popper[8] pointed out that it would lead to solipsism if
one deduces verification from sense-experience and limits sensation to
a particular subject. In fact, Carnap once tended to solipsism of this
kind. Schlick however answered Lewis's criticism by saying that an
antisolipsistic attitude was one of the greatest advantages of true
positivism and that the positivism of Carnap's type was a deviation
from positivism.[9] Be that as it may, "sense-experience not confined
to a particular subject" is an idea difficult to conceive. There may be
two cases in which this idea holds significance. First, when we suppose
a transcendental subject, and second, when we set up a subject-notion
which can be replaced by any possible subject. The first supposition
does not conform to positivism, because if there were any transcendental subject, there would be no reason for it to be sensitive, and no
reason for us to eliminate metaphysics. What remains therefore is the
second case. But in this case, the subject in question will be nothing
more than the logical generalization of sense-intelligible subjects, and
this is conformable to the thought that makes verifiability rather than
verification the canon of meaningfulness.

The possibility of verification is thus regarded as the condition for a

[1] Schlick, *Positivism and Realism*, p. 87.
[2] *Ibid.*
[3] *Ibid.* p. 88.
[4] Schlick, *Meaning and Verification*, p. 148.
[5] Following Popper's Refutations etc. p. 128 ff.
[6] *Erkenntnis* 2, 1923, pp. 222–3, following Popper.
[7] Lewis, C. I., "Experience and Meaning." *The Philosophical Review*, 43, 1934.
repr. in R. Ph. A. p. 128 ff.
[8] Popper, *Refutations* etc.
[9] Schlick, *Meaning and Verification* R. Ph. A. p. 161

proposition to be meaningful. Meaningfulnesss corresponds to verifiability rather than verification, while truth and falsehood correspond to
verification; the one is possibility, the other actuality. The reason why
meaningfulness was referred to verifiability rather than verification is
that verification makes the proposition decisively true or false and if
"meaningfulness" corresponds to actual verification, a proposition
cannot actually be meaningful until it has been decided to be true or
false.

Russell, in his "Human Knowledge,"[1] criticized the verification
theory to the effect that a scientific hypothesis which is generally assumed to be meaningful would turn out to be meaningless. Such a
hypothesis is for example, that there was a time before there were
living beings or that there is iron one thousand yards under the surface
of the earth. This criticism of Russell's was proclaimed by logical positivists to be invalid for the reason that it stands upon the confusion of
verifiability and verification. Russell however did not overlook the
fact that the canon of the logical positivists was the possibility of
verification. He only rejected this thought on the ground that we
cannot definitely know whether a proposition is verifiable or not, since
verifiability contains the knowledge of an infinitely long future. Hence
his witty remark: "that a proposition is verifiable is itself not verifiable." There is some force in Hempel's[2] comment that Russell's objection does not apply because the criterion of verifiability is not an
empirical, but an analytical or a contradictory sentence. Russell however did not consider it to be an empirical sentence. The second notion
of "verifiable" in Russell's sentence indicates the usual meaning
rather than the special one peculiar to the logical positivists; the
sentence therefore implies that we have no way to discriminate whether
or not a proposition is verifiable. Now, if verifiability means that in
case some condition be fulfilled, the decisive verification will happen,
then we must, taking Russell's example, say that a proposition like
"Every man is mortal" is unverifiable, because it can only be verified
after all mankind have died.

Schlick explained the word verifiability to mean verifiable in principle and said that nothing prevents it even if there be no actual verification owing to the lack of technical means. The possibility in princi-

---

[1] Russell, B., *Human Knowledge.* 1948 p. 466.
[2] Hempel, C. G., "The Empiricist Criterion of Meaning." *Revue internationale
de Philosophie* 11 (1950) repr. in *Semantics and the Philosophy of Language.* 1952
p. 166, note.

ple was identified by him with conceivability and logical possibility.[1]
Against the objection that impossibility in principle is hardly dis-
criminable from actual impossibility, Schlick replied that what is
impossible in principle is logically impossible, which differs from empirical impossibility, not in degree but in essence. What is empirically
impossible, according to him, is conceivable, but what is logically impossible is contradictory and inconceivable.[2]

"Possible in principle" is an ambigous concept unsuited to a logical
positivist. The situation is no better even if it be replaced by logical
possibility. If logical possibility is referred to the sentence in question,
most of the metaphysical sentences would be meaningful, because they
usually involve no contradiction in themselves. But if it is referred to
the method of verification, how can we decide whether or not it is
logically possible to verify a sentence? Take for example a sentence:
"There was once a world without life." To verify this sentence one
might suggest a method and say: "One who was alive then, would
have found that there was a world without life." This, however, is
impossible, because it involves a self-contradiction. The original sentence is meaningful, none the less, and it is highly probable that there
is another means of verification which comprises no contradiction. But
the question is, how it is possible to decide whether there is a logical
possibility of verification? One might argue that logical possibility is
directly implied by the lack of logical impossibility. It may be applied
to a particular means of verification, but not to verification in general:
there is no way of assertaining whether a sentence is logically verifiable,
whether there is no logical impossibility at all in verifying a sentence.
This is just what was meant by Russell's remark: "Verifiability is not
verifiable."

In view of this difficulty, Reichenbach introduced another possibility.[3] He enumerated three possibilities, viz., logical physical, and technical. The first means non-contradictory, the second,, non-contradictory
to empirical laws, the third being within the reach of known practical
method. A verifiability defined in terms of technical possibility is
considered to make the definition of meaning too narrow, while a
definition of meaning in terms of logical possibility of verification
is considered to make the definition of meaning too wide, at least,

[1] Schlick, *Positivism* etc. p. 88.
[2] *Ibid.* p. 89.
[3] Reichenbach, H., *The Verifiability Theory of Meaning. Contributions to the
Analysis and Synthesis of Knowledge*, Vol. 80, 1951. repr. in R. Ph. 92 ff.

when the interpretation of physics is concerned. Thus Reichenbach introduced the definition of meaningfulness by physical possibility of verification, but without insisting solely upon this possibility, he admitted three kinds of meaningfulness corresponding to three possibilities of verification. Multiple meanings being thus introduced, it is a matter of course that the criticism of metaphysics loses force to a large extent. Further, there would hardly be any significance in asking whether a criticism is narrower or wider for the determination of meaningfulness. Reichenbach himself admits that none of the three definitions resulting from the three kinds of possibility can be called true, and that none of them seems to supply the only suitable explication of meaning. Now that things have come to this pass, the decision as to what we should admit to be meaningful would be left to one's free choice. The solution of this pragmatic trend will be dealt with later on. Our present concern is with the distinction of verifiability into three kinds: logical, physical, and technical. If there are three kinds of possibility, what is the mark of possibility in general? Logical possibility may well be defined as "having no contradiction," but it is not true with physical possibility, for contradiction is essentially a pure logical relation and there is, strictly speaking, no contradiction against empirical laws. It is true that "All water freezes at 0° C." (S1) contradicts "Some water does not freeze at 0° C" (S2). But (S1) is not the physical law it may appear to be. An empirical law only indicates that water *usually* freezes at 0° C, and there is no contradiction even if it happens that water does not freeze at 0° C. It is at most, an exception from natural law, and the matter is the same even if it may supplied with more conditions such as atmospheric pressure. That water freezes at 0° C, is not deduced analytically from the notion of water, although it is to a degree implicit in the definition of 0° C. (S2) is no less logically possible than (S1). What is then the essence of physical possibility? No satisfactory answer is given on this point. It must be noticed moreover that what is required here is the possibility of verification, rather than the state of affairs indicated in the sentence. There must therefore be three possible cases, namely where the verification is logically possible, where the verification is physically possible, and where the verification is technically possible. Now since verification means stating the condition that makes the proposition true or false, Reichenbach's statement may be formulated: "It is logically (physically, technically) possible to state the condition under which the proposition S is true or false." But with regard to the first formula, it is not clear what is contradictory to what, and what is not contradictory to what. Does it imply that to presuppose A and B in such a way as "If A is B, then S is true, and if A is not B, then S is false" is logically contradictory to something? Suppose for instance we ask whether or not we have memory of our previous life in order to verify a typically metaphysical sentence like "The soul is immortal." Now, in this case, we are not sure in what point the logical contradiction subsists. Unless it is explained, we cannot understand why metaphysical sentences of this sort should be considered as having no meaning.

Next with regard to physical possibility, is it that it is physically possible and does not contradict physical laws to mention the condition under which proposition S is true or false? If physical law is to be expressed as a universal and necessary proposition, it will be *a priori* so, and cannot be distinguished from logical or metaphysical law. But if natural law is of empirical character and cannot be expressed as a universal and necessary proposition, a fact or a sentence that is not subsumed under this law cannot be prohibited as contradictory (to the law). Further, if it be physically impossible to reverse time, it will be physically impossible also to verify the proposition: "Caesar was shaved by his barber on the morning of the day he crossed the Rubicon" with the supposition "If I had been present then, I should have seen that Caesar was shaved etc." (following Marhenke, 153). But if for this reason, the sentence in question lose its meaning, every sentence containing historical facts before our birth would turn out to be meaningless. The sentence, "Stars are holes in the heavens" is false, and therefore meaningful. But how is its verification physically possible? There may be some possible means of verification, but is it necessary for us to reserve the decision as to the meaningfulness of a proposition until we have examined the all possible verifications?

Reichenbach's attempt at setting up a physical possibility of verification between the logical and the technical possibilities met difficulty in finding explicit distinction between these possibilities. And if the limit of physical verifiability is inexact, Popper's[1] suggestion of admitting an intermediate zone of indefinite width between verifiability and non-verifiability, and making natural science gradually diffuse into metaphysics, would seem to be reasonable.

Before Reichenbach, another attempt was made by Carnap[2] to

[1] Popper, *Conjectures and Refutations*, p. 257
[2] Carnap, R., *Testability and Meaning. Philosophy of Science*. 3, 1936 and 4, 1937, repr. in R. Ph. S.

improve the notion of verification. He distinguished testing and confirmation from verification, the former being a somewhat weakened concept of the latter. According to Carnap, verification means a definitive and final establishment of truth, while "we shall call a sentence testable if we know such a method of testing for it; and we call it confirmable if we know under what conditions the sentence would be confirmed."[1] "A sentence may be confirmable without being testable; e.g., if we know that our observation of such and such a course of events would confirm the sentence, and such and such a different course would confirm its negation without knowing how to set up either this or that observation."[2] "A universal sentence, e.g. a so-called law of physics or biology, can never be verified. Even if each single instance of the law were supposed to be verified, the number of instances to which the law refers – e.g. the space-time-points – is infinite and therefore can be never exhausted by our observations which are always finite in number. We cannot verify the law, but we can test it by testing its single instance ... If in the continued series of such testing experiments no negative instance is found but the number of positive instances increases, then our confidence in the law will grow step by step. Thus instead of verification, we may speak, here of gradual increasing confirmation of the law."[3] Thus an empirical synthetic sentence for which the decision as to whether it is true or false is difficult, may be meaningful in the sense that it can be ascertained to be probably true or false. The confirmation increases by degrees, but there is no definite point. "Suppose a sentence S is given, some test-observations for it have been made, and S is confirmed by them in a certain degree. Then it is a matter of practical decision whether we will consider that degree as high enough for our acceptance of S ... the acceptance and the rejection of a (synthetic) sentence always contains a conventional component."[4]

From Carnap's contention, it does not follow of necessity that meaningfulness itself becomes relative and will be entrusted to convention. Therefore it is at least consistent that in spite of his conciliation Carnap held the same attitude towards metaphysics.[5] According to Carnap, the principle of empiricism should be established as a proposal

---

[1] *Ibid.* 47.
[2] *Ibid.*
[3] *Ibid.* 48.
[4] *Ibid.* 49.
[5] In this sense, I do not agree with Popper's criticism. cf. Popper, *Conjectures* etc. p. 274.

or requirement instead of an affirmation in such a form as "All knowledge is empirical" or "All synthetic sentences that we know are based
upon or connected with experience." An empiricist should require
"that descriptive predicates and hence synthetic sentences are not to
be admitted unless they have some connection with possible observation which has to be characterized in a suitable way."[1] With this
supposition Carnap assumed four kinds of requirement:

RCT: Requirement of Complete Testability
RCC: Requirement of Complete Confirmability
RT: Requirement of Testability
RC: Requirement of Confirmability

Of four kinds of language (L_0^t, L_0, L_∞^t, L_∞) which correspond to those
four kinds of requirement Carnap himself is content with the last
mentioned, which is the widest of all. This widest language L_∞ however, according to Carnap, still excludes all sentences of a non-empirical
metaphysics inasmuch as they are not confirmable even incompletely.[2]

We cannot attach much importance to Carnap's emendation of the
criterion, for it is nothing more than a difference of degree, and the
ultimate criterion of meaningfulness was nonetheless sought in sense-
experience. It is very uncertain however why verification or confirmation should have no ground other than sense-experience. Definition is
a matter of convenience. A definition may make meaningful a sentence,
which another definition prohibited. As Popper pointed out,[3] if the
principle of empiricism is not an assertion but a proposal or requirement for selecting a language of science, the attempt to eliminate
metaphysics as meaningless must be abandoned. For the metaphysician neither needs nor would accept such a proposal. He would in its
place, make another proposal according to which metaphysics would
become meaningful. Popper moreover skillfully proved[4] that the
metaphysical assertion "There exists an omnipotent, omnipresent, and
omniscient personal spirit." may be constructed as a meaningful proposition in terms of physical language.

Marhenke,[5] not being content with Carnap's proposal, presented

---

[1] Carnap, *Testability* etc. sec. 18, p. 84.
[2] *Ibid.* p. 86.
[3] Popper, *op. cit.* p. 274.
[4] *Ibid.* 275 f.
[5] Marhenke, P., *The Criterion of Significance. Proceedings and Addresses of
the American Philosophical Association* 23 (1950) repr. in Semantics etc. p.
139 ff.

another criterion of "translatability into usual language." The criterion of meaningfulness is either the definition of meaningfulness or the generalization of meaningful sentences. "A sentence is significant if and only if it expresses a proposition" is the former case, "A sentence is significant if and only if it is verifiable" is the latter. As to the former case Marhenke proceeds by saying that whether a sentence expresses a proposition or not cannot be recognized from the side of the sentence, and that we will commit a vicious circle, since significance is presupposed in the notion of proposition. As to the latter case and with regard to verification, various formulas of verification have appeared since Schlick's first attempt, for example, Marhenke confines his examination to the official versions of Schlick and Carnap. Schlick's first formula was "It is impossible to specify the meaning of an assertion otherwise than by describing the state of affairs that must obtain if the assertion is to be true." From this formulation it appeared that a sentence is significant if it is translatable into a significant sentence. For example, the sentence "Caesar crossed the Rubicon" would be tested by a sentence which uses a different set of words and still describes the same state of affairs, viz., "Caesar went from one bank of the Rubicon to the other."

Schlick says "In order to find the meaning of a sentence we have to transform it by the introduction of successive definitions until finally it contains only words that are not further defined, but whose meaning can be given only by direct ostention." This is transformed by Marhenke: "A sentence is significant if and only if it is possible to specify for every descriptive word that occurs in it a definitional chain (or a set of such chains) whose link is an ostensive definition." This, however, according to Marhenke, is the necessary but not sufficient condition of meaningfulness. Russell's sentence, for example, "Quadruplicity drinks procrastination" can be translated into a sentence which contains only ostensive significant sentence, but is not significant.

Schlick's second formulation: "A sentence is significant if and only if it is possible to specify the circumstances under which the sentence is true" may, in the last analysis, be reduced to the first formula. For the circumstances under which the sentence "Caesar crossed the Rubicon" is true are nothing other than that Caesar crossed the Rubicon, which can be expressed by a sentence such as "Caesar crossed the Rubicon" or some other sentence synonymous with this one.

Schlick's third formula runs: "A sentence is significant if and only if it is verifiable, and to say that it is verifiable is to say that it is logically possible to verify it." But Marhenke points out that Schlick could not show how it is logically possible to verify a sentence, and would in place of it prove that the sentence in question is logically possible, that is to say, he tried to prove that it is logically possible for a river to flow uphill, instead of proving that it is logically possible to verify the sentence that a river flows uphill. Schlick maintained that it is logically possible because the sentence is not contradictory. But he did not state how he determined that the sentence is not self-contradictory. He considered that this determination was made by examining its logical form. But, Marhenke argues, a sentence that is not self-contradictory may be nonsensical, and a sentence may be nonsensical even if neither sentence S nor the sentence which verifies it has any logical contradiction. In order therefore to apply Schlick's test, we have to know in advance that the sentence S is significant. Arguing thus, Marhenke assimilates Schlick's criterion to the effect that we cannot start verification until we know a sentence to be verifiable with the conception that we cannot set the material in a bottle on fire until we know that it is inflammable.

Marhenke further wonders at how Schlick and with him other logical positivists repeating the slogan that the meaning of a sentence is the method of verifying it, have not explicitly thought of what was meant by the method. To verify the sentence; "This is vineger" we may for instance smell the bottle. Now is it really the meaning of that sentence to smell the bottle or to read the label? Schlick actually explained that the sentence about the future are to be verified by waiting for the event to happen, and waiting is the legitimate method of verification. He did not notice that the statements of future events would then turn out synonymous, for they are all reduced to the single method of "waiting."

Schlick's mistake can be explained in sum: As far as Schlick has established the connection between the meaning of a statement and verifiability of it, he used the term verification as a synonym of transformability into a significant statement. If however, verifiability is understood in the ordinary sense as the possibility of describing the method which would ascertain the truth-value of the statement, then verifiability is not the criterion of signifiance, because the method of test or test-sentence can be established only when we know the meaning of the statement to be tested. The decision as to whether the sentence is significant must be made in advance of the testing.

Turning to Carnap, Marhenke continues: "Though Carnap maintained that a sentence is significant when an observation statement can be made that can test the statement in question, he did not use this test when he decided whether a statement in Heidegger's "Was ist Metaphysik?," was a pseudo-proposition, he showed that the statement cannot be transformed into significant statement in ordinary language instead of applying to that statement the criterion of verifiability or confirmability. Carnap's actual criterion should be transformed therefore as follows: "A statement is significant if and only if it is transformable into a significant sentence of standard logical form." Whereas a statement is of standard logical form when it is either a simple sentence or constructible from sentences of that kind by truth-functional composition and qualification. Therefore in order for a statement of standard logical form to be significant, a simple statement must be significant. But there is no criterion for testing whether or not a simple statement is significant, and the decision as to whether or not a statement is significant is, in the last analysis, only possible through a recursion procedure.

Marhenke himself attempts to replace verifiability with transformability into ordinary idiom. The criterion of significance was thus interpreted as transformability into ordinary language or the conversational language of everyday life, which comprises no technical terms.[1] An ironical conclusion indeed for symbolic logicians, parallel to the case of Wittgenstein who after long analysis reached the conclusion that his own sentences were meaningless. Moreover, since it has been demonstrated by many philosophers that it is possible to translate the statements of metaphysicians into ordinary language, the logical positivists' attempt to eliminate metaphysics has utterly failed, and it is highly probable that we shall be led to Popper's[2] judgement that the problem of meaninglessness was a pseudo-problem.

Along with the growing difficulty of establishing the criterion of meaningfulness, the attack against metaphysics has become weaker. The logical positivists at first grasped at some sentences chosen arbitrarily from the works of philosophers whom they did not like and accused them of talking nonsense. But there was no guarantee that the sentences chosen at random represented metaphysics completely, and

[1] Linsky, L., *Semantics and the Philosophy of Language*, Introd. p. 7.
[2] Popper, *Conjectures* etc. p. 258 Popper also says, "The anti-metaphysical bias is a kind of philosophical (or metaphysical) prejudice which prevented the system builders from carrying out their work properly."

the positivists were so excited as to forget the theorem of empiricism to the effect that all empirical knowledge is problematic. They gradually became calm, however, and noticed their hastiness. Still, they preferred not to study traditional metaphysics in order to make a fair judgement upon it. It is as if the logical positivists' *Kritik* is lacking in *Transcendentaler Dialektik*.

Like Kant, the logical positivists found the model of knowledge in empirical science, and considered that empirical knowledge alone has meaning. Hence they sought the criterion of meaningfulness in order to rule out metaphysical propositions. But if actual verification were the condition of meaningfulness, most scientific sentences would turn out to be meaningless. To avoid this absurdity, verifiability instead of verification was adopted as the criterion. This criterion is no less invalid, because empirical sentences are not thoroughly verifiable. Thus confirmability was preferred to verifiability. With all such attempts of improvement, there remains the fatal difficulty that the definition of meaningfulness cannot avoid vicious circle.

For the meaningfulness of a sentence presupposes the meaningfulness of another sentence, so that even if the meaningfulness of the former sentence acquires its foundation in terms of translatability into the latter sentence, meaningfulness itself must be presupposed as an original fact. When the criterion of meaningfulness is found in translatability, it must be reduced to an originally meaningful proposition, or if there be no such single proposition, it must be supported by many other propositions.

A difficulty has been noticed from the beginning as to the meaning of verifiability theory. Wittgenstein was so frank as to admit his own propositions to be meaningless.[1] But this is absurd, because it will make the positivists themselves metaphysicians. Ayer[2] tried to rescue his position by regarding the verification theory itself as a definition. But more sufficient explanation is required in order that this definition should be something more than a mere capricious device. According to Reichenbach,[3] verification theory lays down rules for the construc-

---

[1] Wittgenstein, *op. cit.* (6. 54).

[2] Ayer, *Language* etc. p. 16. In the preface (p. 15) to Logical Positivism (1959) Ayer takes it as convention. But at the same time he has come to admit that metaphysics does not of necessity become meaningless even if metaphysical statements do not belong to the same category as the laws of science and logical laws or as historical narratives or any other commonsense description of the "natural" world.

[3] Reichenbach, H., "The Verifiability Theory of Meaning," in *R. Ph. S.* p. 93 ff.

tion of meaningful expressions, and these rules are conventions determining the structure of language. Being rules, they are neither true nor false, but volitional decisions. Carnap considers that it is possible to make cognitive statements about the properties of the language resulting from the acceptance of these rules and to justify the decision for this set of rules in terms of a certain aim; for instance, the aim of interpreting the language of physics, or the aim of constructing a language that can be used for the purpose of human action. Reichenbach reduces the problem of meaning to the category of explication in Carnap's terminology. It is explained that·explication cannot be said to be true, but can be justified. But, we suspect, insofar as a volitional decision is justified, there must be some cognition presupposed. A rational decision not accompanied by any cognition is a *contradiction in adjecto*. And it is doubtful, moreoever, what difference there is between such a justification and a so-called metaphysical statement. Metaphysics was rejected because its statements could not be verified. And it was said that metaphysical meaning, if any, was not cognitive but emotive. The same thing will be applied to the justification of choice of language. Moreover, justification must mean something weaker than confirmation, otherwise, the choice of language would be either true or false.

The positivists' reconciliation with metaphysics proceeded one step through accepting abstract beings. Carnap[1] and Quine admit abstract entities such as properties designated by predicates and propositions designated by sentences, whereas Ryle attached to this kind of theory such derogatory labels as "Platonic Realism," "Hypostatization," or the "Fido-Fido Principle." The last mentioned is the name given by Ryle to[2] the false inference that assumes a particular entity to which each meaningful expression stands in the relation of designating, just as there is really an entity well known to him. Fido is the name of a dog and the Fido-Fido principle means that there is an entity i.e., his dog Fido, and it is what is meant by the name Fido, viz., his dog Fido corresponding to the name Fido. Thus, the belief that there is always an entity corresponding to each name, exemplified by Fido-Fido, is criticized by Ryle as hypostatization that deals with an expression which is not a name like red or five as a name.

In answer to Ryle's criticism, Carnap points out that there is a fun-

---

[1] Carnap, R., "Empiricism, Semantics and Ontology," in *Semantics* etc. p. 207 ff.
[2] Ryle, G., *Meaning and Necessity. Philosophy*, 24 (1949), p. 69–76.

damental distinction between two kinds of question concerning the existence of reality of entities. In the first place, there is a question as to whether there is in a framework the existence of a new kind of entity. This is called the internal question. In the second place, there is a question as to the existence or reality of the framework itself. This is called the external question. For example, we accept thing-language and the framework of things, and ask whether there is on my desk a sheet of white paper, or whether King Arthur really existed, or whether there are unicorns or centaurs and so on. We may raise or answer these internal questions. And the answer is given through empirical enquiry. It is otherwise with the external question as to the reality of the thing-world itself. This kind of question is not theoretical, but practical, i.e., it is the problem of our language. The decision to accept thing-language does not mean the acceptance of the belief in the reality of the thing-world.

The decision to accept thing-language is a matter of practice rather than theory; nonetheless, it is influenced by theoretical knowledge. The efficacy, fruitfulness and simplicity of the use of the thing-language are the decisive factors. The question concerning these questions is of theoretical nature. But they are not yes-and-no questions, but rather questions of degree. This is the knowledge that the acceptance of thing-language is comparatively useful in everyday life. It is not right to say that the efficiency of thing-language confirms the reality of the thing-world. We should rather say that this fact makes it advisable to accept the thing-language.

Arguing thus, Carnap maintains that the acceptance of a framework is not a metaphysical theory as to the reality of the entity in question. According to him, it is due to a neglect of this important distinction that a modern nominalist like Ryle labels the admission of variables of abstract types as Platonism. If this terminology should be accepted, it will lead to the paradox that he who accepts physical language with real number variables, even if he is a strict empiricist who rejects Platonic metaphysics, would have to be called a Platonist.

Carnap further tries to trace the origin of this distinction in the Vienna Circle. According to him, the Vienna Circle under the leadership of Schlick had already found the non-cognitive character of external questions. For this school rejected the thesis of the reality of the external world and the thesis of its non-reality as pseudo-propositions. The same label is applied to the thesis of the reality of the universal (abstract entities in Carnap's terminology) and the thesis of its non-reality. The apparent negation of a pseudo-proposition evidently is also a pseudo-proposition. Therefore it is not right to assume the members of the Vienna School to be nominalists.

However, Carnap perhaps went too far in attempting to prove new theory. For if the Vienna School had been of the same opinion as later Carnap, how could they have made such an assertion as to eliminate metaphysics? If the acceptance of language were a matter of practical decision, the members of the Vienna School might duly assert that they were not metaphysicians, but would have no right to proclaim that metaphysics was meaningless.

According to Carnap, to accept a framework is a matter of decision rather than theory. He distinguishes himself from those philosophers who regarded the acceptance of the framework as a theory or an assertion. For such philosophers as J. S. Mill, Frege and Russell, Ryle's criticism might be valid. But Carnap considers that they were the same victims of the old metaphysical confusion, whereas he refuses to let his semantic method be regarded as comprising a belief in the reality of abstract entities, rejecting these theses as metaphysical pseudo-propositions.

Carnap at this stage still clings to the beloved expression "metaphysical pseudo-proposition." He seems to indicate thereby the idea that assumes the acceptance of a framework to be a theoretical assertion. Then the thought that admits the non-acceptance of a framework to be theoretical would nonetheless be a metaphysical pseudo-proposition. Thus it would lead to the absurdity that positivism itself should be regarded as metaphysical, and the only possible non-metaphysical theory would be confined to that of Carnap and his fellows who are considered by other positivists rather to tend towards metaphysics. It would be rather against good manners to indulge in terminology with such malicious implications.

To resume, Carnap is of the opinion that the rudimentary problem for those who would develop or use the semantic method is not one of theoretical character as to the existence of abstract entities, but the choice as to which is more convenient and efficient to use the formula of abstract language or to use variables other than for things, this is not a yes-or-no problem but a problem of degree. The adoption of linguistic forms is to be decided by efficiency, and it is worse than futile to inhibit dogmatically a certain linguistic form without testing whether or not it is successful in practical use, because it will be an obstacle to scientific progress. For those who are working in a special field of investigation any form of expression that might seem to be useful for them should be granted. The work in this field will sooner or later lead to the elimination of the expressions which have no useful function. Thus Carnap finishes his treatise with a very generous motto: "Let us be cautious in making assertions and critical in examining them, but tolerant in permitting linguistic forms." It would be more fortunate for us if he were as generous towards metaphysics as he is towards the sciences. However, if the examination for adopting a linguistic form is to be left to each science, there would be nothing for philosophers to be but silent observers. It is doubtful whether philosophers should rejoice or regret being endowed with such a perfect vacation.

With regard to the positivist movement, Daly's[1] remark are most appropriate: "A good deal of this discussion about metaphysics in the last twenty years has been vitiated by the unhistorical and question-begging descriptions given of metaphysics, and by the unfortunate habit of condemning metaphysicians on the basis of propositions torn from their context and understood out of all relation to the immediate argument and the ultimate intention of the author. For Ayer, in 1935, metaphysics seems to have been represented mainly by some of the more paradoxical sentences of Bradley or McTaggart and some of the more tortuous and obscure utterances of Heidegger; but it is not evident that he tried very hard to enter into the minds or discover the intentions of these philosophers."

A more courteous form of ridicule against metaphysics may be found in the label "conceptual poem." In spite of the proclamation under the name of meaningless pseudo-proposition, the positivists felt the need of explaining the historical domination of metaphysics and the metaphysical demand as "a human disposition." Hence Schlick[2] acknowledges that metaphysics makes our life richer and gives us a kind of satisfaction, and calls it a conceptual poem. He goes so far as to admit non-cognitive meaning beside meaning *par excellence*, which is of course cognitive.

Along the same lines Carnap remarks[3]: "Metaphysics does indeed have a content; only it is not a theoretical content. The (pseudo) statements of metaphysics do not serve for the description of states of affairs, neither existing ones (in that case they would be true statements)

[1] Daly, C. B., *Metaphysics and the Limit of Language* in *Prospect for Metaphysics*, ed. by Ian Ramsay p. 178 f.

[2] Schlick, *Erleben, Erkennen, Metaphysik. Kant Studien* XXXI. (1926) p. 158.

[3] Carnap, *Elimination* etc. p. 78 ff.

nor non-existing ones (in that case they would be at least false statements). They serve for the expression of the general attitude of a person
towards life." "Metaphysics is an inadequate means for the expression
of the basic attitude." "Metaphysicians are musicians without musical
ability. Indeed, they have a strong inclination to work with the medium of the theoretical, to connect concepts and thoughts. Now instead
of activating, on the one hand, this inclination in the domain of science,
and satisfying, on the other hand, the need for expression in art, the
metaphysician confuses the two and produces a structure which achieves
nothing for knowledge and something inadequate for the expression of
attitude." The only exception Carnap admitted was Nietzsche who,
almost avoiding the aforesaid confusion, succeeded in expressing his
thoughts either by empirical analysis or in the form of poetry.

Following Carnap, Lazerowitz[1] interprets metaphysics in terms of a
psycho-analytic idea. As he puts it: "Like a dream, a metaphysical
theory is a production of the unconscious and has both sense and moti-
vation. We enjoy it or are repelled by it, it gives us pleasure or pain, a
feeling of security or one of danger; but its meaning is hidden from us.
Just as in our sleep we dream with images so many of us in our waking
intellectual life dream with words.

"A metaphysical theory is a verbal dream ..."[2] "Metaphysics is
linguistic play with a deep purpose, just as a dream may be said to be
mental play with a hidden psychic purpose."[3] "A metaphysician is a
verbal magician who is taken in by his own tricks; he is both subtle
and inventive with words and blind to what he does with them."[4]

However, it is not only metaphysics that is the expression of emotion. The logical positivists themselves depend upon some emotional
motives, as Lazerowitz implies; "It is not easy to dismiss the feeling,
derived from a reading of the literature of contemporary positivism,
that the rejection of metaphysics, though backed by reason, is primarily emotional, an important part of the emotion being shame. The
rejection, one may suspect, constitutes a refined form of book burn-
ing."[5] "Whatever the facts about metaphysics may be, there can be
hardly any doubt that the belief in the positivistic hypothesis has its
main source in the wish to disparage metaphysics."[6]

[1] Lazerowitz, M., *The Structure of Metaphysics*, 1955.
[2] *Ibid.* 26
[3] *Ibid.* 68.
[4] *Ibid.* 79
[5] *Ibid.* 50
[6] *Ibid.* 51.

Lazerowitz' words, without doubt, seem to reveal the secrete of philosophers. It may be true that metaphysical or antimetaphysical theories have their emotive origins. But the problems is whether or not emotion is the only ground of their assertions or rejections; whether or not they are mere expressions of emotion and nothing more. It is true that every action is accompanied by some emotion; still, an emotional act without reason is not worthy of the name of theory. Lazerowitz does not stop at pointing out the emotional concomitants of a theory, he also regards the opposition of metaphysics contra positivism as essentially of an emotional nature. This is to imply that neither the support, nor the rejection of metaphysics has, from a theoretical point of view, any basis, and is left to voluntary decision, or to blind necessity. To be a metaphysician, or to be a positivist would, from his supposition, be left to one's own taste or to fate. Surely, this is the view of an outsider. Suppose for instance, a person who does not understand English is attending Prof. Lazerowitz' lecture. As he does not understand professor's thought, he has to look at Prof. Lazerowitz' tone of voice, gestures, and expressions, and to imagine what is going on in his mind. Now he is informed by his neighbor that Mr. Lazerowitz is talking about metaphysicians and he conjectures from the speaker's smile that the emotions of superiority and pity are the reality behind the professor's attitude towards metaphysics. This connection between emotion and thought is undeniable, to be sure. But it seems to be necessary to inform Mr. Lazerowitz that the reason for his listener's confusion of essence and concomitant phenomenon is due to his ignorance of English. We know that the existence of God and the immortality of the soul were the subjects of *metaphysica specialis*. That these ideas were the expression of philosophers' emotional requirements had, before Lazerowitz, already been taught by Kant. But this kind of interpretation can hardly be applied to *metaphysica generalis* or ontology. We may allow Mr. Lazerowitz to witness a hidden emotional meaning not only in metaphysicians' minds, but also behind the logical positivists' theses, but if even positivism were merely an implicit expression of emotion, philosophy in general would turn out to be merely an emotional expression and nothing more. Thus the emotional theory regarding metaphysics would, in the last analysis, lose its validity. Everything would be left to emotion and taste, including of course the reliance upon and inclination towards science.